DAVID HICKS
LIVING WITH DESIGN

To my father-in-law and in memory of my
mother-in-law with affection and admiration

Other books by David Hicks

David Hicks on Decoration (1966)
David Hicks on Living–with Taste (1968)
David Hicks on Bathrooms (1968)
David Hicks on Decoration–with Fabrics (1971)
David Hicks on Decoration–5 (1972)
The David Hicks Book of Flower Arranging (1976)

DAVID HICKS LIVING WITH DESIGN

in collaboration with
Nicholas Jenkins

William Morrow and Company, Inc.
New York

Designed by Nicholas Jenkins for
George Weidenfeld and Nicolson Limited
91 Clapham High Street
London SW4

ISBN 0-688-03501-9
Library of Congress Catalog Card Number 79-1980

Printed and bound in Italy by L.E.G.O. Vicenza

Contents

□ I have called this book *Living with Design* because this is what I do, whether I am dining with clients, seeing an exhibition, drawing a visual brief for my studio, planting my garden or flying to a design appointment with a sheikh. I think, eat and sleep design in all aspects of my daily life; driving down a street, I criticize the way a woman's skirt hangs, the typography of a pub sign, the new local housing; I question the way a friend has lit a room, how a restaurateur has presented his food. I live with design when I go to the cinema, watch television, arrange flowers, visit a store or an old house, when I help my children in choosing between alternatives – hopefully moulding their sense of design and their taste.

□ If I am reading an historical biography I imagine the way that a seventeenth-century character might have lived and I am fascinated by the details. I know that if he were reasonably prominent he would have slept under a tester bed, and this is one of the things which I have contributed to the scene of interior design over the last fifteen years. In the thirteenth century Yoshida said, 'In all things we yearn for the past.' I have used the past as well as the present for inspiration. I love the past and much of the present too.

□ I am fortunate to have achieved a reputation and as a result to have been asked to design a very varied number of different things : apartments, army messes, art galleries, bedroom slippers, boardrooms, book-bindings, car interiors, carpets, carrier bags, ceramic tiles, china, Christmas decorations, a church, cinemas, clubs, costume jewellery, cruisers, cuff-links, curtains, dress shops, dust jackets, embassies, exhibitions, film sets, furniture, a grave stone, handbags, hotel rooms, houses, imperial suites, interiors for town and country houses, jacquard fabrics, jet interiors, jewellery, kitchens, kitchenware, lamps, landscapes, lifts, lighters, logos, luggage, matchboxes, men's shoes, museums, net curtains, nightclubs, notepads, objects, offices, palazzos, parties, pavilions for meditation, picture frames, picture galleries, plain and patterned fabrics, presentation boxes, pubs, restaurants, roof gardens, royal apartments, scarves, shades, sheets, ships, shoe shops, shooting lodges, silver, ski chalets, socks, suits, sunglasses, tablescapes, theatre sets, ties, towels, tweeds, umbrellas, wallpapers, writing paper and yachts.

□ This is my seventh book and although I still stand by all that I have written before, it will be evident from this book that my experience has widened considerably. I am aware of the need for a more comprehensive book on all aspects of interior design, rather than a book of photographs of interior design solutions. I have noticed that the greater my breadth of practical experience, the more enthusiasm I have for each particular project. Although this is a book chiefly about my work as an interior designer I am, as I have already indicated, deeply involved in the field of product design for the fashion industry as well as interior merchandise. Whereas one day I will be designing an hotel suite, the next day I will be planning a collection of jacquard-weave upholstery fabrics, and the day after a collection of men's shoes. I find the concentration on widely differing fields of design gives me constant stimulation and freshness of approach. My country life and my constant travelling are therapeutic, and my week can, and very often does, include being in or solving problems in Munich, Miami, Mullaghmore, Mittagong or Manchester. I also felt that it might be of interest to include those biographical details that have influenced my attitudes.

□ In this book I have tried to expound a more international approach to interior design, to include the USA, Britain, Europe, Australia and the Far East. In my opinion Americans have, for many years, been the leaders – possibly because they have a great deal more money to spend compared to Europeans. They certainly show a zeal for perfection, and the number of professional interior decorators in America far exceeds that of any other country in the world. Sadly, the Eastern European countries consider good design of any sort to be a totally unimportant aspect of their lives but China may well take a new attitude.

□ The industrial environment is a vast area as yet unconnected with interior design, and I cannot help feeling that factory workers would benefit enormously from interesting and exciting colour schemes and graphics. Cinema and television have educated people in a subliminal way which I believe makes them far more susceptible to good design than they used to be, quite apart from the more positive influence of magazines and newspapers. Office design has undergone a very considerable change over the last one and a half decades and I have been involved in a great deal of it. I show in this book my recent office treatments which have proved to make the environment for the employees very much more sympathetic and conducive to work. I know this is the case with my own office.

□ There are, of course, great frustrations to living design – projects that do not come off for example – but all in all, living design is a great way to live. I can only say how grateful I am to those early clients and product manufacturers who commissioned me and who started the design volcano which will, I trust, continue to erupt for at least another quarter of a century.

My Mother

my father as Master

Myself as Master

My mother in law 1959

☐ The seed of my interest in interior decoration and style was sown by a visit to an extremely boring large Victorian house belonging to friends of my parents, after it had had three rooms redecorated by Geoffrey Holme, then editor of the *Studio* magazine, and Cynthia Eaton. It was a very good magazine and he had what we call taste; he had flair, he had style, he had great originality; so did Lady Eaton.
☐ Holme had taken a series of rather ordinary Victorian family pictures and miniatures, had painted their gilt frames in cream and beige and then rubbed the paint off: he created magic out of almost nothing. He had rehung the pictures in groups and clusters, he had rearranged the other possessions, whether they were stuffed game trophies or visitor's books. All the leather objects were put together on a table and the riding crops were hung as sporting trophies, not just in a row as in every other country house. He had used colour on the walls, colour as I had never seen it used before – blue, I remember, strong cobalt. The impact of that visit, although I cannot have been more than twelve at the time, was very powerful.

☐ I was born and brought up in a cosy, medium-sized house called The Hamlet near Coggeshall in Essex. I became aware of different things, in architecture, in colour, in flowers, in taste, in gardens and furniture at different periods of my life. Coggeshall was an important wool town in the Middle Ages and has a beautiful medieval church which impressed me from an early age, though sadly it was bombed during the war.

☐ It also made me aware of the rather different atmosphere in which my parents lived. My father was born in 1863 and was therefore brought up as a complete Victorian. He ruled the roost as all nineteenth-century gentlemen did. His idea of pictures was a series of hand-coloured hunting prints by John Leech. They were hung along the wall in a straight line in the hall and then up the stairs. Our dining-room was dark red and I remember getting tremendously excited when, in 1938, because my father was getting rather old and took less interest, my mother, catching a slight breeze from the Syrie Maugham movement, had the dining-room painted off-white. She also put up off-white, heavy tweed curtains. Looking back I see that it was a disaster: it didn't enhance the heavy, mid-Victorian polished mahogany sideboards, the Egyptian-influenced marble clock, the cellarets and all the paraphernalia of a Victorian household. The room lost whatever style it had originally had.

☐ Although my father was not very good-looking and had little hair, he had beautiful manners and was a very stylish man. I can remember seeing the reaction of the headmaster's wife when he took me back to my preparatory school and I also remember the effect he had on people on the train. Although we never had much money, he was always immaculately dressed. He had a passionate interest in flowers. Every day for thirty years he caught the same train to the City, to his boring job as a stockbroker, and every day he wore either a home-grown Malmaison carnation when in season, or a bunch of violets in a small silver water-container in his buttonhole.

☐ My father died in 1941. Since my elder brother was away at the war I was alone at home with my mother and so I became rather spoilt. The cars were sold immediately because there was no petrol to be had, and my mother let me turn the garage into a studio. Here I tried out a number of my friend Geoffrey Holme's ideas: for instance, I cut a bakelite washing-up bowl in half and attached the two halves to the wall. Then I put an electric light in them to make indirect lighting. I also got at our picture frames. This was all tremendously exciting to me.

☐ When I went to Charterhouse it seemed like going to Paris after the prescribed perimeters of a prep school. I was a very precocious, unpleasant boy and I made only one friend. He was the son of a famous actor and actress and the fact that we were artistic made everybody else, interested only in cricket and dreadful hockey, seem unsympathetic to us. I spent a great deal of time in the art school. The art master was a pleasant man who let me do 'my own thing', while being a very good guide in the background: he encouraged me when I did something original and never discouraged me. Certainly I always felt that my enthusiasm for art was one of the reasons why I was not much liked at school.

☐ I went straight from Charterhouse to the Central School of Art, having not been allowed even to sit School Certificate because the school said it would have been impossible for me to pass. There I studied painting, book illustration, theatre design, costume design and typography, but I did not work hard at any of these subjects although I think I did learn to draw. In those days I had no idea what I really wanted to do or to be. Sometimes I saw myself becoming a prominent West End actor, designing sets for my own plays which I would also write and direct. I also imagined myself as John Piper, Graham Sutherland and Henry Moore, all rolled into one superstar English artist, and I actually did rather good drawings in their three different styles. As John Piper I was greatly interested by churches and as an art student I was never out of museums and houses which were beginning to open to the public. I was, I think, the youngest member ever of the Georgian Group. I would steep myself in historic buildings, absorbing the atmosphere, the look and the feel of places, all of which was for me a very important part of the gradual process of my becoming an interior decorator and interior designer. As Graham Sutherland I did romantic semi-abstract landscapes and as Moore I did mountainous nudes. I certainly learned perspective although perhaps I really taught myself that. I have always delighted in good drawings and ever since my days at the Central I have surrounded myself with architectural drawings, not only because the subjects are architectural but because I love the way they have been rendered. I greatly appreciate the effect of a soft pencil on rough cartridge paper or a fine nib on very fine paper. It is all part of my absolutely dedicated interest in clean lines and pure design. I see university and art school as a period for reflection and rumination – really a time to sort oneself out. I think one learns very little from other people – one really teaches oneself. I certainly did.

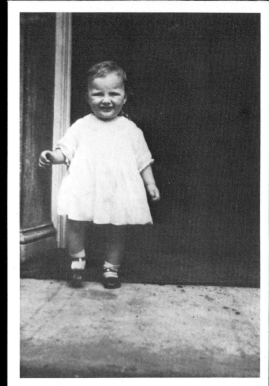

☐ I went into the army from art school and then went straight back to the Central School after the army. I was totally unsuited to being a soldier but I managed to get myself into the Royal Army Education Corps and I taught art to band boys of the Royal Engineers at Chatham. In fact I was a hopeless disciplinarian, I just sat in the corner and did my own thing and let them do theirs – which was mostly reading comics.

☐ Nostalgia to me is one of the great pleasures of life, and I even like going back to the scene of my old army barracks at Chatham and Folkestone. I look back on those times as miserable, cold and uncomfortable, and the people with whom I had to live as raucous, vulgar, smelly and dreadful, but it still gives me a certain pleasure to remember them perhaps because I escaped from them.

☐ Other patches of nostalgia in my service life were release courses at Welbeck Abbey in the underground ballroom built by the fifth Duke of Portland. Because we were the Education Corps we were considered civilized and allowed to use the magnificent library. It had been re-housed in about 1910 and had an Edwardian plasterwork barrel-vaulted roof. The library contained the most stunning, rich, superb collection of Edwardian leather bindings, together with a number of important early bindings.

☐ The first place where I was stationed in the army was Buchanan Castle in Scotland. It has now been pulled down, but then it was in the most magnificent setting. All the furniture had been removed from the house but it still had fantastic nineteenth-century stained-glass windows and turrets. What a contrast between that and going on weekend leave to Glasgow, staying the night in a third-rate boarding house in Sauchiehall Street and trying to go to sleep with the noise of the trams rattling up and down outside. But what a pleasure to be able to go to look at leisure at Charles Rennie Mackintosh's Glasgow School of Art and then have tea in the famous tea-rooms also designed by him.

☐ After art school I travelled for a year; I went to Spain and Italy, and stayed with a family in France. I was still trying to make up my mind what to do. My mother thought it was inevitable that I was going to live in London and so decided to sell her house in Essex. In 1953 she bought a house in South Eaton Place, which she let me redecorate entirely as I wanted. I had a temporary job in advertising in the art department at J. Walter Thompson; I loathed it, but it tided me over the six months while I was doing the house, and I think by that time I knew I was going to be an interior decorator. The house was photographed by *House and Garden* and in the week the article appeared three prospective clients rang up. Overnight I became an interior decorator.

☐ In fact it was the climax to a series of incredibly lucky events. I asked the right person, Peter Coats, who was an editor for *House and Garden*, for a drink to see the house. They happened to have a photographer free. And pictures of the house appeared in the magazine almost immediately. One of the people who telephoned was an American, Mrs Rex Benson, who had been married to Condé Nast, the founder-proprietor of *House and Garden*. She happened to like me. It is a difficult thing to say but I think charm never hurts. I was after all totally inexperienced and I knew nothing about interior decorating, so she was taking a big risk. But she was a woman of great taste herself and together we decorated her new flat. Perhaps it was because of that very happy first job, working with a client, that I have always maintained that the interior decorator and the interior designer must be the interpreter of their client's taste, their style and their way of life. They must not be dictators and I have tried never to be one. At about the same time I redesigned the glass and china department at the G.T.C. through a childhood friend, Elizabeth Everard.

☐ My first commissions in 1955 were a huge success and led to many others, for my client knew people like Douglas Fairbanks Jr., Mrs Gilbert Miller and Earl Beatty. They all asked who had done her new flat and gave me lots of small jobs like re-covering a sofa or making a pair of curtains. Afterwards I was given a yacht to do, then a drawing-room, then a complete flat. The work snowballed.

☐ At the end of the year, I went into partnership with Tom Parr, an antique dealer, and opened my first shop, Hicks and Parr, in Lowndes Street, Chelsea. Sitting in an office waiting for word-of-mouth contacts to telephone is time-wasting : having a shop window generates business. Tom now runs Colefax & Fowler – a highly successful interior decorating firm – whose work I admire greatly. In 1959 I started David Hicks Ltd in Lowndes Street, but in 1963 I closed my shop and worked from a house in St Leonard's Terrace ; I also worked a lot in the United States.

☐ My organization and shop are now at 101 Jermyn Street, London SW1, and are headed by my brother-in-law as chairman, a managing director and a financial director. I have a chief interior designer, a chief product designer and several designers and draughtsmen working under them. I am under contract to twenty-one Japanese companies, to two carpet manufacturers and three furnishing fabric manufacturers. I have associates and shops in Switzerland, France, Belgium, Pakistan and Germany. Twenty-five years later it is no longer a matter of making one pair of curtains.

D. N. Hicks

There has been some impro

I think, but it is not enough. He m

in hand.

I have been impressed by what

of his work in Studio.

...ent in his work,
...t really take himself

...ave been

Birley

Headmaster

my father

In Italy in 1951

My father shooting, watched
by Mrs J. Arthur Rank

1950

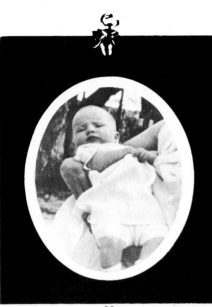

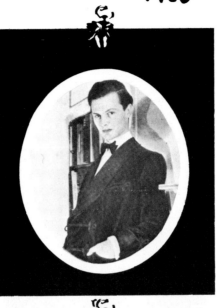

in the R.A.E.C in 47

1952

Case history:
A country house in Oxfordshire

□ I first saw Britwell Salome, a country house in Oxfordshire, when it was advertised for sale, with a photograph, in *The Times* in February 1960. My wife and I had no intention of buying a country house, we had only married in January and had not yet finished doing up our small flat in Lowndes Street, but my mother-in-law had just died so any interest to keep our minds diverted from that great sadness was important.

□ Going up the drive at Britwell we were immediately captivated by the most extraordinary sense of calm, of beautiful country and fine old trees. Looking back I saw a landscape that appeared to be one of the most untouched in the whole of England – it could not have looked very different in the eighteenth century. Turning a bend in the drive we were confronted by a column erected, as I later discovered, in 1764 by Sir Edward Simeon, the builder of the house, in memory of his parents. The column had a nostalgic compulsion for me because I grew up near two grand houses in Essex, one of which had a column in the park. Columns

□ One of the first things I did when we moved into Britwell was to claw off all the Virginia creeper from the back and front of the house and plant climbing roses and *Vitis coignetiae* to reclothe it, but only partially. Although I like Virginia creeper very much, it should always be reserved for areas and surfaces which face north, and it should always be controlled. Houses big or small, flats, garden walls, garages and outbuildings are all much improved if they have plants growing over them, but romanticism must not go too far. A classical house in particular should never be smothered.

had always been a status symbol which I found irresistible.

☐ When we first saw the house it was in a rather bad state and the south wing had had some additions which we later pulled down. On entering the hall I was overwhelmed by the extravagant English baroque stone chimneypiece surmounted by a vase of early eighteenth-century plasterwork flowers. Then, after seeing endless charming rooms, we went into the dining-room which had been built in 1768 as a chapel; the concave, oval plasterwork ceiling, the columns, the fact that the room was oval itself and had an oval stone floor, totally convinced me that we could not go back to London without saying that we wanted to buy the house, although we had no idea whether it was within our means. My wife was more intrigued by the two nurseries in the attic with their vast semi-circular windows. Although the house had been hideously painted in a dreadful jade green and had unsympathetic furniture in it, I could see what it could become with the right kind of colour and furniture – a conversation piece of early eighteenth-century gutsy architecture. And in fact it proved to have the happiest atmosphere of any house I have known: although it is quite large, one could sleep in it completely alone and yet not feel in any way uncomfortable.

☐ The original house of 1728 was the square block in the centre. The oval chapel was a totally independent building of 1768–9 built by Sir Edward, a recusant, and was connected in about 1790 by quadrants to the two pavilions. Later still another addition, which

contained the priest's room, was put on between the main block and the chapel. So in fact the house is of four distinct dates. All four façades are dressed with Oxford stone coining, and the window frames are in the same stone.

☐ Having bought the house, we started work on the main block. There are certain basic things you do as an interior designer when you look at a space or a series of spaces which need redesigning, renovating or restoring. I knew at once that the hall had to have a very stony feeling and I suspected that, many coats down, the wall surfaces would reveal the original colour. Under sixteen layers of paint I discovered a rather gentle, bronze colour which I then recreated. I used a dragged brush technique which I felt was in sympathy with the stone and slate floor, for the doors, cornice and dado. I based the decoration of the staircase hall on a document of an early eighteenth-century woven blue-and-white cotton damask. Although only two-thirds of the repeat existed, with my studio I worked out the last third of the repeat and this was printed as blue-and-white wallpaper in Vienna, because at that time nobody in England could print wallpaper with the wet-look technique, which

emulated the fabric well.

☐ It took nine months to restore the house. Having made certain basic decisions I went away with scale drawings and elevations to Australia. On one of those incredibly long flights I spent hours, thousands of feet above the Philippines or wherever we were, drawing out details. Mostly I was working on the north wing which had originally been a farm building, only converted in 1924; it was a veritable beehive of rooms which needed considerable sorting out. I think now that we spent too much money on this reconstruction, because we never used the wing as much as we thought we would.

☐ The stable building was in a bad state of repair and originally contained a very low-ceilinged bothy for unmarried gardeners. As I wanted to make a service flat there I let down the floor; this still meant that the ceiling of the garages below was high enough for modern cars although, of course, it would have been much too low for eighteenth-century carriages.

☐ It was most unusual, even in 1960, for a couple as young as ourselves to buy such a large house. While our trustees were very interested in the land that went with the house, they were horrified at the thought of the running costs.

They also felt it would be detrimental to my profession if it were known that I lived in such a grand house. I was thirty. In fact, quite the reverse happened. I was determined that it would not be an interior decorator's showpiece. I did not want the rooms to look like over-dramatic or unnecessarily photogenic showrooms. But because I have a feeling for the different atmosphere of different rooms with different uses, the house became a catalogue of the versatility and catholicity of my taste and my outlook on the treatment of rooms. Yet it was also a real country house. It never ceased to be one of the best selling assets for me as a professional adviser. It is probably one of the most photographed private houses in the world.

☐ Certainly it was a very big undertaking. Luckily in the 1960s wages were very much lower. We started off very grandly with a chef, a butler, a footman, a housekeeper, a housemaid, several 'dailies' and a Fellow of the Royal Horticultural Society as head gardener. We had hothouses in which we did extraordinary things with plants – for instance we grew bananas that fruited, I had five-foot-high hollyhocks flowering in pots in the house in February, and *Campanula pyramidalis* in July which were at least seven feet high. All white and massed in a corner, they looked like glittering, snow-covered Eiffel Towers.

☐ When we first bought Britwell, we had a minimum of furniture. It mostly either came from my wife's London flat, or was lent by my father-in-law. We also had the contents of my London house and my weekend folly in Essex – an eighteenth-century fishing pavilion on a canal. There was nothing like enough to fill the house. Although I bought a large piece of furniture and several objects practically every week, it was a very large house to fill. I initially conceived the house to look like an early eighteenth-century conversation piece by Hogarth or Arthur Devis. Paintings of eighteenth-century interiors show them as very underfurnished. They nearly always have very dark or very light walls : there is nothing wishy-washy about them. The painting of Roger Newdigate in his famous gothic library at Arbury in Warwickshire shows some very elaborate gothic bookcases stuffed with rare books, but there is just one piece of furniture – a reading desk.

☐ The *Country Life* articles on great country houses, published between 1900 and 1930, which are

to me a great source of pleasure, recorded these houses photo-graphically – some medieval, some Carolean, some eighteenth-century – at a period when probably three or four other great houses' contents had been inherited by the owners, on top of which they had all the veneer of Edwardian and Victorian clutter. The historic houses which are now open to the public are, generally speaking, slightly less cluttered. They have been edited down a bit, but they are still basically much, much fuller than they originally were.

☐ So I arrived at quite an exciting, stark look at Britwell and early photographs in 1961 show it comparatively underfurnished. But then we started to inherit furniture, I am also an inveterate buyer, and gradually the house became the cluttered, cosy, full house that it ended up being in 1978. With relish I spent six months deciding what I would take to our new set of rooms in London, what to the dower house in the country, and what to my wife's family house in Ireland. I now have a great feeling for an uncluttered look in the country, and because my last flat in London was very modern and very stark, I am now in the mood for a very full, very rich, 1830s look in my new rooms

in Piccadilly.

☐ In the late 1960s inflation began to rear its ugly head. The process of cutting down the staff was a gradual one. The first person to go was the footman, and it was sad no longer to see polished brass buttons and the butler in white tie and tails. But, of course, the fewer people you employ the simpler life is ; and although we had lived in a pretty grand way in the early sixties, right from the outset I had tried to be practical. I had, for instance, installed a house telephone so that we could ring the groom to say when we wanted to go out riding.

☐ The glories and eccentricities of the garden had to be curtailed. The situation was succinctly and dramatically illustrated by the family accountant who came to lunch one July day. For dessert we gave him one of our home-grown bananas ; he cut it very exactly into twelve pieces and when he had eaten it he said, 'That was a delicious banana, but I am afraid that it will have to be the last one to be eaten in this house as it cost £49.50.' So that afternoon I told the gardener that he would have to turn off the heat in the tropical house. Britwell was a wonderful house with an extraordinary view and we loved living in it.

Case history:
A country house in Oxfordshire

☐ To enhance a statue silhouetted
against a pre-war yew hedge, I
planted two lines of instant lime
trees which I planned eventually to
pollard.

□ Rhubarb: more delectable when growing than, in my experience, it can ever be for lunch on Sunday.

Case history:
A country house in Oxfordshire

□ At one end of the terrace there is a vista looking through to the Chiltern Hills. I felt that the other end needed a focal point to balance it, so I placed there a metal stag, which is identical to the pair at Bowood in Wiltshire.

□ On top of the stable I built a belfry which I modelled on that of a local eighteenth-century church at Chislehampton. This housed the Britwell bell which always used to be rung at nine o'clock at night and six in the morning before the Great War to tell the villagers when to go to bed and when to get up. It was also rung on Sundays for Mass. I put my H logo on the rusticated wooden base.

☐ When trying out new vases I use breeze blocks to form temporary bases so that I can judge the proportion.

☐ The garden, apart from the walled rose garden, depends very largely on mown lawns, gravel and lines of trees.

☐ I bought the centre-piece of the rose garden in a local builder's yard. It was originally the base of the lightning conductor at Blenheim Palace; it is made of cast iron, and must have been put up, judging by the design, in about 1790. The large ball which surmounts it is the original finial and I surmounted it with two ballcocks which I gilded.

Case history:
A country house in Oxfordshire

□ The sunk garden, where we had a swimming
pool built, originally contained a lily pond which was
too small in scale for the area, and herbaceous
borders, which I detest. As a foil for the pool I
designed a geometric planting of beech hedging and
clumps of bamboo against a background of yew. I
planted the spaces in the recesses with all green plants
– pyramids of bay, spirals of box, rhubarb, Portuguese
laurel, artichokes, rheums and a carpet of bergenia.
□ When we bought the house the grass on the great
lawn on the west side of the house was waist-high;
the lawn had been planted with evergreens in the
nineteenth century so there was a tremendous amount
of reclamation to be done. At a slightly later stage I
decided to put in a canal which also acts as a reservoir
against fire, and on either side I planted two lines of
clipped chestnut trees, giving importance to the
centuries-old oak in the centre of the vista.

Case history:
A country house in Oxfordshire

☐ Pierced doorways, gates and railing, all of different periods and styles, add enormous interest to a large garden when carefully integrated with their surroundings.

☐ A view from the yellow cotton-covered batchelor room into its adjoining bathroom, where I covered the walls with one of my small geometric wallpapers and hung engravings of classical buildings in a formal pattern over the mahogany-based bath.

□ The bath in my bathroom at Britwell was placed in the middle of the room. The field of the beige and white painted panelled walls was in *faux granite* on which were hung drawings and paintings. The carpet was my first geometric design, inspired by mosaic decorations on an early mosque which I saw in Persia in 1960. On the bath is a mahogany reading stand.

☐ The library is a square room with a high ceiling. The walls are painted matt black, the ceiling and woodwork white. The roman shades at the windows are made of grey flannel with a darker grey inset border, and the carpet is one of my geometric designs in black, white and grey. I managed to find a simple marble chimneypiece, contemporary with the house, to replace the Victorian one which was there when we moved in.

☐ The desk is Edwardian and comfortably copious with plenty of secret locks and drawers. It was made for the great Edwardian financier, Sir Ernest Cassel. The red leather cushion was made for his motorcar.

☐ I am in the process of having my favourite books rebound in maroon, aubergine and scarlet leather. Small, vertical, standing brass lamps were directed towards clusters of red-bound books grouped together to give the feeling of a red library. I hope that by the end of my life all my books will be bound in red.

Case history:
A country house in Oxfordshire

□ The curved picture gallery has Indian cotton on the walls, a varied assembly of nineteenth-century furniture, and coconut matting on the floor. Portraits, engravings and photographs are massed on the walls.

□ The quadrant below the picture gallery housed busts representing four continents – Asia, Europe, Africa and America – in bronze-painted terracotta, probably dating from the early 1800s. I designed the mahogany and ebony bases on which they stood. The tables hold a clutter of wooden boxes collected by my mother. Reproduction brass and green glass-shaded library lamps give an atmospheric light, as does the uplighter underneath the octagonal relief plaque which came from a Nash house in Regent's Park.

Case history:
A country house in Oxfordshire

□ As a landlord, I have always
been extremely interested in the
buildings which we own on the
Britwell Estate, and have restored,
renovated and even built cottages.
When a porch, for instance, has to
be added on to a house for practical
reasons, I consider its design very
carefully. It is unusual for anyone
involved in farming to pay much
attention to the appearance of
barns, cottages or houses – but I
had a grain dryer, for instance, built
in a stock asbestos of dark
aubergine which fits into the
countryside far better than the
monstrous off-white ones which
most farmers choose.

☐ From my earliest years I have always had a tremendous feeling for estates. I have noticed that a number of landowners, large and small, use house styles – whether it be the colour of their cottages' front doors or a family crest – to denote ownership. So I put the H logo on the two farmworkers' cottages and the farm manager's house, as well as on other cottages which we own.

Case history:
A country house in Oxfordshire

□ When decorating Britwell I thought it essential that each of the bedrooms should have a very different atmosphere.
□ Only the main beam existed in this visitor's bedroom: I added subsidiary ones because I wanted to create a suitable environment to house a collection of early oak furniture which I had inherited from my mother. The bedcovers on the half-tester bed are in a gold, tan and beige Victorian flower print on a black background. The floor is covered wall-to-wall in coconut matting, the curtains are Etruscan red tweed, and an early nineteenth-century Turkish cotton rug hangs over the bedside table. All the pictures belonged to my parents and date from about 1910.

□ This bedroom has white-painted panelling and a white ceiling, and the interior of the tester bed is lined entirely in white glazed chintz. The bedspread is made of the same material but quilted, with the H logo all over it. I used one of my American sheet designs to cover the exterior of the bed, and for the curtains and pelmets; the design of the pelmets was inspired by a late seventeenth-century original in the castle of Skö Kloster in Sweden. I designed the emerald-green carpet with a white carved pattern specifically for this room in 1960.

☐ I devised this tester bed to hang from an elaborately moulded wooden tester bolted on to the ceiling beams, and covered it in an eighteenth-century French printed cotton copied from the original *toile d'Aix.* The interior of the bed is off-white shantung, and the pelmet and leading edge of the curtains are trimmed in maroon. An eighteenth-century raspberry silk damask cushion is placed in an armchair covered in the same material as the bed hangings. The picture to the right of the bed is fixed to a jib door: because I wanted to centre the picture on the panel to balance the one to the left of the bed, I cut through the picture and its frame so that part of it opens with the door and part remains on the wall. It was not a good picture.

☐ For this bedroom I made a tester bed, and I tied the corners of the pelmets with small bows made of the same cotton that covers the walls. The interior of the bed is a blue-and-white polka-dot cotton. Two eighteenth-century brass candlesticks have been electrified to make practical bedside reading lamps. There are two white-painted English elbow chairs in the French style, and the carpet is a very inexpensive off-white cord.

Case history:
A country house in Oxfordshire

□ In collaboration with the architect Colin Golding, I recently designed an octagonal house for a minute piece of land which we owned in the village. I have always been intrigued by octagonal, oval and circular houses; in England there are a great number of toll houses and lodges which are octagonal, and there are some follies built in the other shapes.
□ The house has an octagonal living-room/dining-room with a central chimney which is open on both sides. The left-hand pavilion is a tiny study and the right-hand one is the kitchen. The staircase is at the

back, leading to the first floor
which contains two bedrooms and
a central bathroom. The carpet is
one of my earliest designs –
octagons interspersed with
diamonds.
□ The windows are regular mass-
produced sash windows; the only
ones available now are four panes
wide, whereas, in the past, three
panes have been more usual, and
the proportions of the house were
dictated, to some extent, by the
availability of these standard frames.
□ We sold the house on the basis
of a drawing and a plot with
building permission.

Case history:
A country house in Oxfordshire

□ I had the original eighteenth-century floorboards in this room relaid to follow the octagonal shape of the room, and I designed an octagonal area rug. In the centre was a partly-decorated Worcester vase sitting on a fine Regency pedestal table.

□ The panels in this room were painted in grisaille by Rex Whistler for my mother-in-law in 1937. Fortunately she insisted that he painted on canvas rather than straight on to plaster, which he usually did, so she was able to move the panels away from her Park Lane penthouse at the beginning of the war. The arrangement of the panels here is completely different from the original one because the rooms are of different dimensions.
□ The Louis XVI table with a white marble top held a collection of eighteenth- and nineteenth-century European and Russian boxes and white porcelain.

On the walls of the drawing-room I stretched a simple English linen of white and buttermilk and made the curtains in the same fabric. In order to understate the cornice – it dates from about 1829, the original having been destroyed by fire – I painted it out white with the ceiling. The carpet is a very subtle beige cotton which blends well with the cream silk velvet-covered Louis XVI *bergères* and the Louis XVI *canapé* covered in pale pink. The paintings are all modern, and a collection of blue objects is displayed under the lamp. To my mind this room, which was used by dogs and children and people coming straight in from the terrace, had a marvellously relaxed yet civilized feel.

Case history:
A country house in Oxfordshire

□ The dining-room at Britwell was originally built as a chapel by Sir Edward Simeon and was completed in 1769. When we bought the house, the room had a dirty white ceiling and muddy jade green walls. I repainted them a deep claret and used brilliant scarlet Braintree silk for the curtains and tablecloth, which was covered with a plastic cloth and a top cloth of red and white cotton. Two wing chairs were covered in crimson silk velvet, and the chandelier chain was bound in the silk damask of the curtains. On the stone floor I used an oval felt rug in a deep red with a dark brown border. I painted the

architectural woodwork in a very pale stone shade to contrast with the pure white ceiling and cornice.

□ In the evening I lit the hall with uplighters placed in each corner of the room, which threw into dramatic relief the architectural detail of the frieze and the circular-headed architrave. Whenever possible, if it was at all cold, I liked to have a fire burning there because I think it is one of the most welcoming sights in the world. The tall-backed chair was one of a pair in the hall which are entirely painted in grisaille except for the coat of arms. They are extremely rare and were made in about 1689 for Holme Lacey, a house belonging to the Stanhope family in Herefordshire.

Case history:
A country house in Oxfordshire

□ Although the house had a
drawing-room which was fine for
about eight people, we needed a
larger reception-room for
entertaining, so I knocked two
rooms into one to create a second
drawing-room. But it was not just a
room that was used only for a large
party – I have spent a great deal of
time there on my own listening to
Wagner very loud late at night, and
for this reason I put in an acoustic
ceiling so that the visitors sleeping
above would not be disturbed.
□ I wanted to create a very
colourful, young-looking room
because our other drawing-room is
classical and blond. The only other
red room in the house is the dining-
room which is a deep claret and
quite different from this.
□ The objects in the room are very
disparate. The red sandstone horse
is modern but in the true Mogul
tradition; it was carved in Agra, in
India. The group of *papier mâché*
figures in the corner was made by
three Spanish sculptor-painters
called El Equipo and was modelled
on the painting of Carlos IV and his
family by Goya. In this group,
however, the queen holds an Irish
leprechaun in her arms and wears
the Union Jack as a dress.
□ I bought the Andrew Yates
painting over the sofa specifically
for this room, although I think it
would look just as well in a white,
beige or yellow room. It appeals to
me because the absolutely regular
geometric theme is broken in a
subtle way by the interesting
placing of colour in the rectangles.

Case history:
A London flat

☐ I was asked to create a pale, simple, feminine background for a collection of Chinese antiquities, modern paintings and graphics in a rather unprepossessing pre-war London flat.
1. I covered the walls of the living-room in an off-white textured fabric, and the floor with one of my sculptured relief carpets in three shades of beige. The banquettes are upholstered in pale pink raw silk with cushions in various shades of rose pink.
2. In the dressing-room I used blue tweed for the walls and sofa bed and I placed an eggshell-blue lacquer commode that I designed under a blue and chromium mirror. The patterned fabric on the chair works interestingly with the carpet design.
3. I used sycamore and beech flush panelling on the dining-room walls, placed beech grilles over the windows to conceal their metal frames and the radiators beneath them and placed a glass-topped writing table at one end of the room, while the dining table itself has a sycamore base with a glass top. The traditional rope chairs come from Italy. The carpet in salmon, sand and white and the banks of oval spotlights coming from the ceiling give the room a warm, sunny feeling.
☐ Each room has its own ambience and colour theme but the flat is united by a soft beige hall, staircase and landing.

1

2

Case history:
Chambers in Albany

1

3

2

4

□ Albany, or Albany House as it is properly called, was built in 1774 for the first Lord Melbourne, my wife's ancestor, father of the Prime Minister, and was originally known as Melbourne House. In 1803 a Mr Copland bought the house from the Duke of York and Albany, who had called it York House, and got permission to rename it Albany House. He made it into chambers and, at the same time, commissioned Henry Holland to build two terraces in Lord Melbourne's old garden behind. These buildings, three storeys high with an attic, became the first apartments or flats in the world.
□ Ever since I decorated a set of chambers in Albany in the 1950s I had wanted to live there. When I moved my offices to Jermyn Street, which is five minutes' walk away, my desire became overwhelming. Living there is like living in an Oxford college: acres of mahogany handrails on iron-balustraded staircases; total

quiet and privacy. It probably has more style than any other set of apartments in the world.
□ Very little change has taken place in my chambers since 1804. The original detail had been retained but the front door, which had been redone in about 1870, needed replacing so I had the carpenter make a flush panelled door to Henry Holland's design.
1/2. The bedroom before and after redecoration. I removed a cornice from the top of the built-in cupboards of the thirties and applied a chair rail to the wall: after redecorating the cupboards have become a dramatic and unexpected support for the urns which are lit by concealed lighting. The wall-to-wall carpet is in orange, yellow and brown with a complementary border. The festoon curtains are always kept at the height shown here and the mid-nineteenth-century standing desk in front of the window helps to obscure the view of neighbours.

3/4. The small bathroom half-way through redecoration and when completed. I thought it needed a crisp and stylish treatment so I used one of my newest designs both for the wallpaper and the curtains under the vanitory unit. I used two pieces of mirror reaching to the ceiling to create an illusion of space.
5/6. The drawing-room after and before redecoration. I painted the walls a matt Venetian red and hung eight oval portraits, each with its own picture light. The *Directoire*-style swan chairs are covered in scarlet tweed, and the Louis XV chairs in puce tweed.
7. I always have either a vase of flowers or, in winter, leaves on a brown snakeskin-topped table in the drawing-room.
8. A Louis XVI-style *bonheur de jour* holds a nineteenth-century bronze electrified candlestick, a bunch of dried hydrangeas, two Lowestoft saucers and a late seventeenth-century drawing of a battle scene.

5

6

7

8

Case history:
A country house in Ireland

☐ Four years ago some young clients, who had taken over a large part of their historic family house in Ireland, asked me to rethink their way of living in the deep countryside, not only for the 1970s but for the 1990s too. My solution was to create an all-purpose family room in which they could eat, sit, cook, have the children playing and watch television. It also serves as a bar, a laundry and flower room. Each activity has its clearly defined area. But it remains one large entity. Built in the 1780s, the house had always been a family one and therefore had to be practical. To my mind it needed a certain element of Victorian pattern on pattern on pattern, as well as bright modern colours and strong lighting. I tried to retain the atmosphere of the house while at the same time giving it a feeling of today.

☐ To warm the staircase hall I used a rich scarlet on the walls and individual lights on the family portraits.

□ The long gallery floor is covered wall-to-wall in jute matting – an unexpected, inexpensive covering which makes an excellent foil for the fine eighteenth-century furniture. For the ten windows I designed an enormous damask pattern which I printed in white pigment on a simple beige cotton. I hung the gathered pelmets with their thick wool fringe from the original carved white and gilded curtain pelmet poles. The large lilies and other plants growing in tubs by the windows are excellent in scale for a room of this proportion.

Case history:
A country house in Ireland

□ One of my first suggestions was to convert a very grand, large dining-room into what has become known as the family room. I created eight areas where the family can eat, cook, drink, wash up, arrange flowers, read, listen to music and watch television. This is the room which the family use when they are alone or entertaining up to eight visitors; the rotunda is used for larger lunch and dinner parties.

☐ The only daylight in the rotunda came from a circular skylight in the domed ceiling. I used a warm buttercup yellow for the walls, picked out the frieze in pale lettuce green and painted the coffered ceiling in four different greys. I lit the pale green scagliola columns from behind with downlighters, and the alcoves, which hold a collection of porcelain, with parabolic spotlights. A circular carpet was woven for the room in Manila. The permanent tablecloth of green glazed chintz has a wadded contrasting green edging at the base.

Case history:
A country house in Ireland

A detail of one end of the gallery shows the walls painted pale beige with the mouldings picked out in white. I electrified the kolser oil chandeliers and put them on rheostat switches, while the wall sconces were de-electrified and real candles are now used in them. I covered a pair of fine eighteenth-century gilded chairs in pale pink suede cloth.

In the library I picked out the frieze in white with a scarlet background, painted the inside of the bookcases in scarlet lacquer and re-used the old dining-room velvet curtains to cover the walls above the bookcases. The carpet is a gothic quatrefoil design which I scaled up for this room. There is a *trompe l'oeil* door painted with false books behind the Chinese black and gold lacquered screen which was originally made for this room. I found an eighteenth-century wooden chimneypiece from another family house in the cellar and re-used it here.

☐ I had always had the urge to get
back to my roots in the country for
that was where I was born and
brought up. My parents were both
keen gardeners and my father was
an extremely good shot. When we
married in 1960, my wife and I
decided that we would eventually
make our main home in the country.
We bought the Britwell estate
which involved a considerable
acreage of farmland, and since I
had always ridden and gardened
for pleasure, riding round the farms,
shooting and gardening became
again an essential part of my life.
We have farmed in partnership with
two highly professional farmers
ever since.
☐ All this is in strict contrast to my
city life as a designer. I find that I
cannot work to order in the
country. I often take papers down
with me to read at the weekend and
a sketchbook so that I can do some
designing, yet by Monday I have
done absolutely nothing because I
have been preoccupied by
weeding, pruning, garden planning
and other country pursuits. But I
always have a notepad with me
whatever I am doing, whether I am
riding, shooting or gardening.
Suddenly I will think of some detail
– a hotel room in Tokyo perhaps, or
the solution for an awkward corner
in a showroom in Munich – and I
will jot it down.
☐ I bitterly resent the inroads
continually being made into our
once sacrosanct countryside. We
are very fortunate to live in a part of
Oxfordshire that is still very
untouched, but for how long? The
road which we border on is now a

continual stream of lorries far too big for it; pollution is everywhere.

□ Another quite different aspect of my life is that of a liveryman of the Worshipful Company of Salters. The City of London Livery Companies originated in medieval times when they had the power to control and inspect the members of their respective trades' products. The Salters formerly dealt not only in salt but in sugar, spices and ale. Today the company has charitable and educational functions only, providing funds for research and scholarships in the field of industrial chemistry and looking after almspeople. My father, grandfather, great-uncle and many cousins were all Masters of the Salters. I became a liveryman by patrimony. Some years ago I was invited to be a member of the court and in 1977–8 I was Master of the Company. Although I know little about industrial chemistry, I am interested in education and in the other aspects of the Company's charitable activities. When the Company's hall was rebuilt in 1976 I was on the committee which dealt with the interior design and the result has been acclaimed as the only good modern livery company hall. The architect was Sir Basil Spence.

□ I find that having two, if not three, totally separate lives is extremely invigorating because one returns to design situations, colour and taste, furniture and lighting, with rejuvenated energy, not having concentrated on them for a few days.

A holiday house

☐ In 1967 we bought some land on the island of Eleuthera in the Bahamas, and decided to build a house there for our own use at Easter which we would rent out for the rest of the season. When I was in Egypt in 1961 I was enormously impressed by the remains of the tomb of Zoser at Sakkara which is one of the earliest surviving stone buildings in the world. So with the architect, Robert Stokes, I designed a contemporary house in concrete, taking the Egyptian tomb as our inspiration.

☐ Two pylons by the entrance serve absolutely no function whatsoever except to make the view more dramatic. The house is literally built on the sand; it is held down by a water tank buried under it which is as large as the entire building. The windows of all the bedrooms are at the corners of the house, and only the living-room has two windows, placed on either side of the chimneypiece.

☐ The internal walls throughout were finished exactly as the external walls, in rough concrete heavily mixed with the pinkish beige sand from the beach. I used the simplest and least expensive of furnishings: white roller blinds at the living-room windows; simple bedspreads of my own design in the bedrooms; and a large square of coconut matting in the drawing-room. It is still, after twelve years, a simple but immaculate house.

Astronauts in the David Hicks
Suite at the St Regis Hotel –
New York

the family
with
Bertie

off to a party
1968

India, aged 1

Edwina and Ashley

☐ Before considering interior decorating and designing today it will be useful to look briefly at the history of the professions. In the eighteenth century you might commission a new London house, an addition to your house in the country, or rebuild your house from scratch. My brother-in-law's family did just that in the 1760s: Robert Adam was commissioned to design the new house and the furniture to go with it. The furniture was made by Mr Chippendale and his workshop and is still in the family's possession.

☐ At that time the architect would not only decide on the structure of the house, but also choose the interior finishes. He ordered the silk damask for the walls, he designed the furniture, he told the upholder (so called because he originally upheld tester beds) what to put on the chairs, and he designed the floors whether stone, wood or carpeted. He was interior designer and architect rolled into one. He was an interior designer, not an interior decorator, because he was actually designing and creating the furniture and furnishings.

☐ This system continued into the nineteenth century. William Porden in the 1820s rebuilt Eaton Hall for Earl Grosvenor. He designed the exterior and interior architecture, and the furniture. Later in the nineteenth century came William Morris, who was a furniture and fabric designer and an interior designer, probably one of the first who practised as such since Daniel Marot, who worked in Holland, England and France in the late seventeenth century.

☐ In the 1920s we find architects resuming their eighteenth-century role of designing not only the building, but the appurtenances of the interior as well. Simpson's of Piccadilly was one of the first modern commercial buildings in Europe, built in 1935–6, and the architect, Joseph Emberton, designed not only the exterior but all the interior finishes, and the furniture, display stands and rugs as well.

☐ Early in this century, in America, Edith Wharton wrote her famous book on interior decoration. In England Syrie Maugham, known by her friends to have taste, was asked with increasing regularity to advise on their houses and flats. Concurrently in Paris Elsie de Wolfe was making many contributions to interior decoration; it was she who fixed the light switch at its present – to my mind correct – height of thirty-three inches from the floor. There were a number of men and women acting as advisers on interior decoration and it began to permeate the large London houses and New York and Paris apartments. In America the profession grew and grew so that at the end of the Second World War there were probably more than 30,000 interior decorators.

☐ The interior decorator and the interior designer are two rather different professions today. The interior decorator, generally speaking, deals with the private sector: he changes the colour of the walls, re-covers the furniture, rearranges it, relights the room, puts in a new chimney. The interior designer works more usually in the public sector – in hotels, offices, restaurants and other areas for which furniture is specially designed. In the private sector he is working as an interior architect and is designing furniture, fitments, cornices and spaces from scratch. They are really comparatively new professions. Very few interior decorators are interior designers, but many interior designers are also interior decorators.

☐ There is a general feeling among the public that interior decorators, as opposed to designers, are people who waft into a room saying 'Pink ceilings and blue walls', and waft out again. There may be a number of amateurs who do just that, but in fact it is a very serious profession and extremely hard work. Anyone can dream up an attractive colour scheme or pick out a beautiful eighteenth-century table, but to get a house with six bedrooms completed on time within a fixed budget takes much more than flair: it requires a really tough, efficient, business-like attitude backed by all the right services.

☐ There has been a massive increase in demand for interior decoration. Until the *nouveaux riches* appeared as a result of the Industrial Revolution, and in this century with the post-First World War manufacturing boom, rich people lived in inherited houses with inherited possessions. But the *nouveaux riches* were building new houses or buying old houses from people who could no longer afford to keep them up, and they had no confidence in their ability to put a home together. They wanted to reflect their new-found status and they needed the confidence of a professional to tell them not only what to live in but also how to live. I have often dealt with foreigners who come to London and are anxious to find out how we live here: they want advice on the kind of glass to choose, the kind of china, how to set the table, etcetera.

☐ Interior designers have a very real use in people's lives because they are thinking all the time about the problems of proportion, of texture and lighting, and of making atmosphere, and are therefore continually gaining experience from which their clients can benefit. They are also very good at furniture arrangements so that they can usually make the best use of space. I know many people who have never employed an interior designer whose houses, lifestyles, decorations and collections I admire tremendously; they have probably more taste than a number of professionals in certain areas. They do not need an interior designer, but most people do: it is a definite professional advisory need equivalent to seeing your doctor when you are ill or a dentist when your teeth hurt.

☐ As an interior designer I consider myself to be an interpreter of my client's taste. My first question to a new customer is: 'Do tell me, what have you thought of doing?' An English person immediately understands the question, although Americans and Europeans sometimes look a little puzzled: they want to be told what to have. Very often one does a marvellous, immaculate interior and then says to the client: 'Now this is the background. We do not want to buy everything at once, but you, over the next two or three years, must go out and bring your own personality in by buying more pictures or objects.' Of course, they sometimes buy the wrong ones and they hang or place them badly. The placing of objects and the hanging of pictures is very important.

☐ There are, however, times when a client follows the designer's original concept to a degree which is totally inhuman and ludicrous. I once redecorated an apartment for a woman in New York and on one of my visits, when I had nearly finished, she asked me to buy some flowers for her. I went out and spent $100 on what I thought were the right flowers for the time of year (June) – lilies and carnations – and arranged them on the chimneypiece. When I came back to New York eighteen months later I rang my client and asked if I could come to see the apartment. She asked me to come in two days' time, and when I arrived I was astonished to see pink carnations and white lilies identical to the ones I had bought eighteen months previously. They had been flown in from somewhere warmer. And when I suggested a change in the arrangement on the chimney, in moving a vase I found underneath, painted on the marble, a very fine white circle where the maid had to replace the vase every day after dusting.

☐ I have had no radical shifts of attitude to interior design over the years, rather an evolving, ever-widening view. I have gone into new forms of lighting, of upholstery and fabrics. When perspex or plexiglass first appeared I took it up with enjoyment but I used it with a great degree of restraint.

☐ My major contribution as an interior designer has been to show people how to use bold colour mixtures, how to use patterned carpets, how to light rooms and how to mix old with new. Many people have influenced me in all these directions, and a number of designers have been working parallel to me in other countries.

☐ I believe that the real reason for my lasting success is that I have always avoided using gimmicks. I have always been very disciplined and I have never used anything new, strange or revolutionary without very careful consideration. The Englishness that people like in the way we live is typified by a cosy, relaxed look. I may create a very disciplined background but then I like things messed up or cosied up a little. I am always thinking of warmth, of practicality – where the children are going to watch television for example. It is this which really gives what I have done for people a sense of it being theirs rather than merely the concept of an interior designer.

☐ When my first job was about ten years old, my client rang me up and said, 'I would like to see you because the flat has got dirty and I want to re-do it.' I replied, 'Oh good, because I have some marvellous fabrics and carpets and all sorts of things designed since I did the flat for you.' 'Oh, no,' she said. 'You don't understand. I want it exactly the way you did it ten years ago.' It was boring – but flattering.

☐ I have had some disasters in my time. I once designed a very elaborate modern book table for an Australian client's set of Audubon books. There were six volumes, 3 feet by 2 feet, so the table was not suitable for anything else. The top was plate glass, under which you could open one volume and display a plate. The client was shown drawings of it and accepted the estimate, but when the finished table arrived she would not let the delivery man in. I still have the table.

☐ I designed a restaurant in the King's Road in London entirely in black and white except for the carpet, which was a brilliant splash of colour. Geometric shapes echoing the carpet – obelisks, rotundas, pyramids, cylinders and spheres – were painted in black directly on to the white walls. Unfortunately, a couple of months after the restaurant opened, the owner rang up and said, 'We are simply not getting any customers. The room is too cold.' So I then went and coloured in the shapes and, alas, the result of that was really much less stylish.

☐ There are a number of people working in my field whom I admire. In England I was a great admirer, during his lifetime, of John Fowler and I think that Tom Parr has succeeded brilliantly in continuing the Fowler tradition. Jon Bannenberg is an exciting, very modern, rather brutal interior designer. People like David Milinaric, John Stephanides and Tessa Kennedy are doing very interesting interiors. But perhaps Terence Conran has made the greatest contribution. I am full of admiration for his work and could very happily furnish several houses from Habitat.

☐ Since all my previous books are now out of print I believe that my work must still be appreciated, in spite of a review which I received for my first book in *House and Garden* in 1968: 'Mr Hicks now seems to feel the urge to make rules for others – his rules – but it just isn't on. . . . Long before he is middle-aged, Mr Hicks' current notions and dicta may well seem fairly *vieux jeux*, even to himself.' I still stand by all that I said in that book and I do not believe that my ideas have become out of date. I have had a number of protegées who have almost without exception become successful in their own right – Mark Hampton, William McCarty, Carla Venosta and Fiona Armstrong, to name but four. What to me is really rewarding is that we have worked on projects together, have reached design solutions together, and that when they have gone out on their own they have respected what they learnt from me but have made their own very personal contribution to good interior design.

☐ With experience and some degree of success, it is easier to convince clients of the proposals that I submit than it was in those early days when I had little achievement to back me up. I found my ventures into fashion particularly challenging because I was right back at the beginning again and I had to struggle to put my ideas over. Once again I had no previous experience or success behind me.

☐ In my fiftieth year there are still many design fields that I would like to work in and I have every intention of attempting them. In the meantime I am content to have been involved in such a wide variety of design contracts.

Live with a touch of class

PERSONALITY
Jane Fraser

"WHEN PEOPLE like you ask me what the new colours are for the season, I simply refuse to say a word. I mean, good lord, I might be committing a young couple to 10 years with a red or purple drawing room. I think it's utterly immoral!"

Mellifluous voice edged with pain, he draws his eyebrows over his nose, purses his lips and does press-ups with his fingers, palm against palm.

This is the urbane Englishman, David Hicks, speaking on decor in his Johannesburg shop and about how YOU too can live with a bit of class — Hicks class.

"The whole emphasis is on understatement. People must be educated to recognise this. Understatement has been the hallmark of good taste ever since the war . No-one with taste overstates. Well," he says with an almost imperceptible shudder, "gaudy people do. I mean, I've NEVER seen an actress with a beautiful home.

"Never use gimmicks," he says sternly.

How can we do it? How can we achieve the metamorphosis from tat to taste effectively?

You can do it piecemeal, as long as you have an eye for the complete whole. "It's no good getting a couch that later won't go with curtains that won't match......" he explains.

David Hicks uses cotton or calico, gingham or coconut matting in the right circumstances.

"Certainly move the furniture around occasionally. At the window consider 'dress curtains', that don't actually pull and use blinds in a pretty design.

"I 'did' a house for Vidal Sassoon way back in 1958. He only had R100 in the bank." He says this with more than a measure of satisfaction. David Hicks loves a challenge.

He has been known to cover a couch in navy and white gingham, use unbleached calico as curtains.

For table lamps his suggestion is to cover the existing shade with an extra "skirt". A small length of patterned fabric gathered to fit the top of a cone-shaped shade can just hang down to the edge of the shade.

Another quick reviver for a tired room is to make a table-cover from a piece of felt in a bright zingy colour.

Make use of the furniture you already have and don't go for fashion for fashion's sake. Remember no gimmicks.

It sounds so easy, doesn't it?

David Hicks . . . "the emp[hasis]
statemen[t]
PICTURE Vikki Perei[ra]

Mr Hicks lan[ds] on the pron[gs] of a devilish dilemma

DAVID HICKS

Mr. David Hicks, whose rapidly expanding busin[ess] interests include a directorship of a firm of eatin[g] houses, is not content to confine himself to the directo[r's] chair. He has lent his talents to designing a 25ft.-lo[ng] trident as the firm's coat-of-arms.

But his enterprise has u[n]expectedly landed the com[pany in a spot of bother.

When workmen arrived to erect the sign in front of the firm's newest branch in Kensington a startled worshipper shot out of nearby St. Mary Abbots Church.

"You can't put that up there —it's the sign of the Devil." he insisted.

Not sure

Now Mr. Peter Evans, the head of the firm, has received a tart letter from Kensington Borough Council . . . .

It is considered that the sign, in particular the excessively large representation of a fork, is inappropriate and injurious to amenity having regard to its position immediately adjoining the cloistered entrance of St. Mary Abbots Church.

Said Mr. Evans: "I wasn't sure whether to fall down and gnash my teeth in anger or burst my sides with laughter when I heard about it. I think I did both."

Determined

But Mr. Evans, who wants to illuminate the sign at night, is a very determined man.

He has sent an appeal to the Minister of Planning, and the sign is going up today regardless.

"After all. it cost me £1,000 one way or another," he told me last night.

STEAK SIMPLE
SCAMPI SPECIAL
FOOD UNSURPASSED

PETER EVANS
EATING HOUSE

THE WICKED FORK

How David Hicks went to the wall

SAY David Hicks and people immediately think: Decor. More than any other British interior designer he has managed to put over his certain style.

Seldom has he used flowers as a motif. However they do pop up, side by side with his favourite geometric patterns and dramatic, almost heraldic designs, in his latest venture; a collection of wallpapers for Coloroll.

Counties

All the papers have been named after English counties. I've chosen 'Yorkshire' twice for the showhouse.

It's a zig-zag design based on an old weaving pattern, in a blend of muted pink, cream, pale almond green and a subtle, sludgy brown.

In the playroom the same pattern is almost unrecognisable recoloured in strong red, yellow, green and blue. 'Cheshire' is the paper that puts Hicks flowers on your walls. Again I've used the same pattern twice to demonstrate the astonishing difference a change of colour scheme can make.

Hexagon

Naturally you'll find a hexagon design in the collection called Oxford. Maybe it's an unusual choice for a bedroom, but I love the exotic effect of a trellis of olive green framing small hexagons of vivid parrot green.

On the hall stairs and landing there's an elegant combination of cream brown and Best Beige.

All the papers in the new Coloroll David Hicks Collection cost £2·50 a roll (plus VAT), 11yds. long. Selection available soon from Debenham Stores.

The pet hates of David Hicks ..

QUESTION to newly-weds and about-to-be-marrieds: Is there a three-piece suite of easy chairs and sofa in your home-making plans?

If there IS—perhaps you should think again.

For according to top interior decorator David Hicks, who married Lady Pamela Mountbatten, the traditional three-piece is BORING.

He advises: "Buy a sofa in one colour and two chairs in another."

He knows . . .

Mr. Hicks, who is consultant designer to a chain of furniture stores, certainly knows what he likes—and dislikes.

Here is a list of his pet hates:

Wooden bedheads (he likes covered foam-rubber bedheads);

Splash marks on painted bathroom walls (plate glass at strategic places on the walls helps);

Embossed wall paper;

Stained glass panels in a front door;

Plastic curtains in the kitchen (try washable venetian blinds);

WE were impressed by Mr. Hicks. We liked his homely approach to home-making:

"Decorating in certain circumstances can consist in merely rearranging existing furniture in a room. . . ."

Or, "I think it's very important in redecorating not to throw out everything. You must evolve a scheme around your treasured possessions."

WE asked Mr. Hicks the kind of questions that worry every new home-maker.

● Mr. David Hicks

Q: What is the first essential in a new home?

A: Floor covering. If you decide on wall-to-wall carpeting don't stint on quality. Choose a neutral colour to last for years and suit several colour schemes.

Q: Are you in favour of the open-plan dining-kitchen area?

A: To do this elegantly is beyond the reach of most people. But a glass partition between the cooking department and eating is one solution.

Q: How many coloured areas can you have in one room?

A: Keep down to two colours — such as four walls and a different ceiling, or three similar walls with toning wall and ceiling.

☐ Taste is a particular person's choice between alternatives. It is choosing a tie to go with a shirt to go with a suit to go with an occasion. It is the way you arrange oranges in a greengrocer's shop; the way you light your room; the colour you choose for the outside of your motor car. It applies to food, to interiors, to manners, to anything where it is a question of choice between one alternative and another in connection with colour, style or behaviour.

☐ There is a certain stratum of people around the world who consider that they know what a good choice of these elements is: this is what has become known as good taste. Thus you have what is generally considered to be good taste in pictures, good taste in gardens, good taste in interiors, and conversely you have kitsch taste, theatrical taste, vulgar taste and common taste.

☐ The international *cognoscenti* elect themselves over the generations. At the end of the nineteenth century John Ruskin made tremendous proclamations about taste which you cannot really argue with today: he was right within the context of what he was preaching. In the 1900s Edith Wharton was regarded as a paragon of taste. People like Syrie Maugham and Elsie de Wolfe were regarded as leaders of fashion and style in interior design in America, England and France in the late twenties and thirties. History has not, on the whole, proved them wrong.

☐ Taste is not something you are born with, nor is it anything to do with your social background. It is worth remembering that practically anyone of significance in the world of the arts, whether in the past or today, was nobody to start off with. No one has ever heard of Handel's or Gainsborough's father.

Nepotism and parental influence count for little in the history of talented designers, architects, painters and musicians. Good taste is something which you can acquire: you can teach it to yourself, but you must be deeply interested. It is in no way dependent upon money.

□ Many things are palatable to those of us who are supposedly people of taste, but then they are copied and become vulgarized by misuse; through association with their misuse they become unpopular with us. But I am always open to revivals – it is just a question of reusing something in the right way. There was a time in my life when moiré or watered silk was absolutely intolerable to me, but I now find it acceptable because the mass of vulgarians have moved away from it; now I can reintroduce it and reuse it in a sympathetic way. There was a time when I loathed vermicelli quilting – it used to be done by pathetic lady decorators on watercolour chintzes of no character whatsoever. But now I like it and use it. It must be done on plain chintz though, and not on a patterned fabric. One reason why I like it so much now is my deep interest in rustication in architecture, a theme which has played a very important part in classical and baroque architecture throughout the centuries.

□ There is in fact an acceptable way of using almost everything. If someone asked me to design a room for them, but confessed that they collected gnomes, I would make a gnomescape on a table. If someone had a passion for flights of ducks I would say that I would use not just one but nine flights and would arrange them in a Vasarely-type way, painting the ducks black and white alternately.

Reproductions

☐ Reproduction furniture is a difficult area. There are reproduction tables and chairs where the manufacturers get the basic feeling – the line is right and the proportions are right – but they antique or varnish them and spot them with little false woodworm holes; or paint them off-white with gold paint brushed over the embossed bits of pseudo-carving, all of which I find totally unacceptable. I sell absolutely brand new traditional chairs of seasoned wood either lacquered or with just the right degree of polish on them. I also sell new tables of traditional design with similar finishes. The essential point about reproduction furniture is that it must have a clean, honest finish. It must not be pretentious in any way. Although it looks tremendous when it is new and will do so in two hundred years' time, it will need to be cleaned down and re-polished, lacquered or repainted after twenty-five years.

☐ I totally disapprove of reproducing canework on tin, or simulating marble on linoleum, yet I love eighteenth-century marbling, *trompe l'oeil* architectural detail, scagliola porphyry, graining, jib doors and marbelized pottery. The latter group are acceptable because, being hand-made, they have individual quality, warmth and wit, which marbelized linoleum lacks. This is not to say that I dislike printed tin or linoleum – on the contrary, I am fascinated by modern materials but they must be properly used.

☐ I do not approve of coloured reproductions of oil paintings on canvas-textured paper. If a client said to me that he loved Van Gogh and wanted to use a series of coloured reproductions of his paintings, I would say no. I find a straightforward facsimile of a black-and-white drawing acceptable because it is very close to the original, whether it is an engraving, an architectural drawing or a landscape. There are also excellent sculptural reproductions of antiquities to be bought in museums.

Maintenance

□ To keep interiors in good condition can be an expensive business – it depends how much one is prepared to put into it oneself. One of my great relaxations is washing things : as soon as I arrive at my house in the Bahamas I get some hot water and soap and wash all the objects, glass table tops and picture glass.

□ Loose covers can, of course, be dry cleaned and tight covers can be sprayed with a protective product. I find that a lot can be cleaned off tight covers by breading them : one simply gets a crust with some crumb on it and uses it on the chair like an india-rubber.

□ Wooden floors can have a polyurethane coating to obviate polishing and stone floors can be washed or varnished. Carpets can be cleaned on site and even interlined curtains can be dry cleaned, though one must remember that an elaborately draped pelmet would have to be dismantled before cleaning and reassembled afterwards. Curtains with cord controls soil less quickly than ones without. Wallpapers can be coated so as to be spongeable and fabric-covered walls can be cleaned with a vacuum cleaning attachment.

□ Silver, brass and copper can be lacquered to prevent tarnishing, but do not do this to good old silver. Smoking fireplaces are often improved by fixing a section of toughened glass to the top of the opening. A fireplace which smokes when first lit but not later can be cured by sending several large sheets of newspaper alight up the chimney to create a warm draught just before lighting the fire. However, never do this in a house with a thatched roof.

□ An old lampshade can be given a new look simply by making a skirt of gathered fabric and stitching it to the metal frame of the old shade.

Quantity as quality

☐ I am inclined to begin with a room looking very bare but, being an inveterate collector, I nearly always end up with a good deal of clutter. It is not a question of what you do but how you do it which adds up to style. Even in a hotel room I unpack all the books and sketch pads that I travel with, put them on a table and arrange them, but then I am an arranger by nature.

☐ My passion for arranging masses of things together is part of the way that I see objects and use them. It not only looks mean, but is visually meaningless, to have one bottle of gin, one of whisky, a couple of tonic water and a soda syphon on a table in the living-room, even though that might be perfectly adequate for the needs of one evening's entertainment. I like rows and rows of tonic water bottles, apple and tomato juice, two or three syphons, and several back-up bottles of spirits lined up behind each other; it gives a generous, welcoming atmosphere, and if a bus-load of friends does descend upon you, you are ready for them.

☐ If you are going to have a table with photographs, you must have enough of them: the more you have, the more interesting the table will become. In the illustration to the right there is only one photograph displayed, inscribed to us by Sir Noel Coward, but it is backed up by books, a number of circular boxes and some pieces of cable which were laid in 1865 under the Atlantic between England and America. They were given to my grandfather who was a shareholder in the company concerned.

Everyday objects

□ Even the most ordinary, everyday objects benefit from careful arrangement. When I buy grapefruit or oranges I arrange them in a large pottery bowl to be a decorative feature until they are consumed. I arrange utensils in our kitchen with a sense of design; I buy soap which will go well with the colour scheme of the bathroom. One can enhance one's life visually all the time if even the simplest things – the way magazines are put out on a table, logs stacked, suits or dresses hung in a wardrobe, gum-boots lined or cassettes stored (mine are in perspex boxes stacked on top of each other) – are arranged with style.

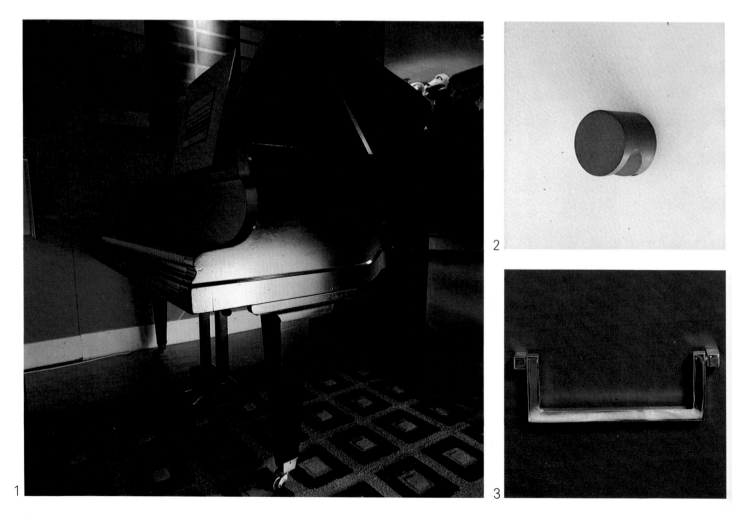

1

2

3

1. A grand piano can be a very decorative object but uprights need redesigning. This piano, which we inherited from a great grandfather, had hideous, bulbous legs. I replaced them with some new, square-section tapering legs and re-finished it in eggshell lacquer.

2. A handsome modern cylindrical doorhandle, part of a range which I specify whether it be for a new apartment or an eighteenth-century house where the original accessories are missing.

3. A drawer handle which I designed for desks and commodes has a pure, simple elegance.

4. The television set has probably caused interior designers more problems than any other everyday object. The most successful solution that I have found is to place the set directly on the ground under an antique or modern table. One views it from a sofa or chair at much the same angle that one would watch a film from the dress circle of a cinema.

5. This red telephone, designed and made abroad, is to my mind an interesting attempt to create a new look in telephones, although I dislike the two plastic labels above and below the push-button dialling and I find the handpiece too angular. The best modern telephones are the pure white ones in the United States; the worst are those to be found in England, particularly the two-tone terrors.

6. An old-fashioned spray and tap.

5

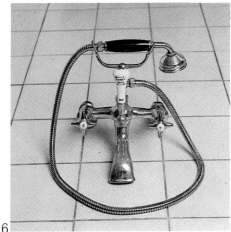

6

Colour

☐ Colour can achieve more effect in people's lives at less expense than any other element in interior decoration; a coat of paint can totally transform an area. Colour can change mood and atmosphere – it can make a room warm, gay, receptive, subtle, soft, hard, classical or bizarre. You can do a great deal with colour but you cannot make a room look taller by painting the ceiling white, or lower it by painting the cornice white and the ceiling off-white – it does not make the slightest bit of difference.

☐ I have always had a passion for what some people consider clashing colours. I call them vibrating colours – for instance, vermilion, shocking pink, puce, salmon pink and blue pink. I like them with aubergine. All reds go together, and I include both pink and orange in the red family.

☐ At the moment I am going through a deep, rich, earth-coloured phase but I cannot allow this to dominate or affect the work I do for my clients; I must use a very impersonal colour palate. Clients always have very special colour preferences and for this reason I try initially to discover from the people for whom I am working what their favourite colours are so that it is their colour scheme not mine. But I monitor the scheme to ensure that the result is what they like and at the same time has my approbation – after all, they have consulted me as an expert in the field of design and colour.

☐ Certain climates need certain sorts of colours. Northern Europe demands a different palette from Southern Italy, though both cool and hot climates benefit from accents of colour which can change seasonally. This is easier than it sounds, for one can cover scatter cushions in winter or summer colours and make loose covers for alternative seasons reasonably inexpensively. A sofa can be tight-covered in a dark,

1

2

3

warm, practical winter colour and can be transformed in late spring with a paler, loose cover ready for summer.

1. There are very many different blacks and whites. In this illustration a black-and-white carpet, white roman shades with black trimming, white stools and curtains, with pools of intense light from parabolic spotlights, together create a dramatic background for a fashion showroom and show how effective a non-colour scheme can be.

2. A small, second living-room with aubergine tweed on the walls. The traditional, serpentine-backed sofa is covered in a darker aubergine, and massed with cushions in glazed chintz of related, vibrating colours. A Louis XVI-style chair has an unpretentious, pure beech finish which has merely been polished.

3. The colours of the Indian dhurrie on the floor work well with the blues of the tables, chairs and sofa, the yellow lamp and the modern French *bergère* chairs.

4. The colours of the walls, curtains, carpets, chairs and sofa have been carefully co-ordinated to create an intensely warm and inviting, all-red living-room. The horse's head is modern and from India.

5. The painting by Denis Wirth-Miller on this living-room wall pulls together the blues of the sofa and the lapis lazuli-topped table.

6. The pastel colours in this room are based largely on the Indian dhurrie on the floor. They show how pinks and puces can be used with cornflower and cerulean blues against an off-white background.

6

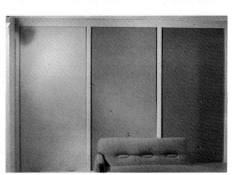

□ I created the internal architecture of this London restaurant which was once a Covent Garden warehouse. Over the square central section we made a Pantheon-like domed ceiling, and in the section beyond deep coffers, all of which had daylight coming through top skylights. Parabolic spotlights cast interesting pools of light on the walls, which are covered with Brussels weave carpet, and on the sliding red lacquer grille screens.

□ Wherever possible I like to recess the ceiling lighting fully; in this instance I was able only partly to recess the downlighters but they still make an interesting regular pattern on the ceiling.

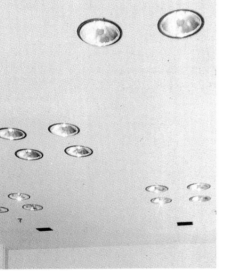

□ Groups of four parabolic spotlights are placed regularly in the ceiling to give extra interest to an otherwise dull ceiling surface.

□ In an open-plan office I highlighted the beams by running strip lighting parallel to them.

□ When I am confronted by a period house or building, I nearly always leave the ceilings as I find them; usually I paint them white, although there are exceptions to the rule. A lot of nonsense is talked about bringing a ceiling down by painting it a special colour. I find high ceilings even in very small rooms extremely pleasing. Sometimes, because of awkward structural beams in a modern building, I will use a false ceiling; more often than not it will be a floated ceiling which enables me to use fully recessed light apertures and air conditioning. A floated ceiling obviates the necessity for a cornice, which is useful when working to a strict budget, as is so often the case. I have designed a number of complicated ceilings, particularly in restaurants and other public areas, using strongly painted beams and dramatic coffering specifically to give atmosphere and dramatic interest.

□ Period cornices can be rerun by taking moulds to make up missing sections and whole cornices, friezes and chair-rails can be commissioned. Alas, standard cornices are very poorly designed and it is a great pity that no manufacturer has thought of mass-producing good traditional and modern cornices, as well as other architectural details, in glass fibre.

□ Any form of light-fitting hanging from the ceiling is anathema to me with the exception of chandeliers, which can be traditional or modern but must be lit with great sensitivity. In a modern interior I like to stud the ceiling with parabolic spotlights; I do this occasionally in period rooms if there are structural beams which can be featured, or to add character to a room.

□ A short and rather narrow staircase in my London headquarters is given importance and scale by the illusory perspective of the flanking screens.

□ I like to see a piece of furniture, a lamp and some objects on a staircase landing if it is at all possible, since staircases tend to be empty and boring.

□ For a house in Spain my associate there devised a heavy architectural treatment for a change of level involving four steps and a built-in banquette seat which gives a feeling of airy freedom to the space.

□ It seemed important to me that this circular staircase should end up in an inviting way to people approaching it from right or left. I therefore made it twist out in both directions in the eighteenth-century manner, although I used totally contemporary detailing for the handrail and surrounding architecture.

□ The architecture of this building demanded a dramatic change of level, so I made a feature of it. I carpeted the stairs but the living-room has a white tiled floor as a background to a rug.

□ An extra sleeping area was needed in this room so I made one out of extra space and fixed an access ladder to the door and the wall above.

□ On this staircase I used a brilliant tangerine carpet, and for the walls a very strong geometric design of mine printed on hessian. I made a feature of the elaborate circular thirties window.

☐ I have always been fascinated by the way, in the past, that doors were concealed, whether for aesthetic or practical reasons. There are many examples of different periods. Instances can be found at Versailles, the Ephrussi de Rothschild, the Villa Viscaya and in English country houses. In England we call them jib doors. I create them very often.

1/2. To conceal two large doors opening into the library at Britwell, which interrupted the intimate atmosphere, I used a false screen of four panels with two of the panels attached to each door: when closed, the doors are totally unseen.
3/4. In a study, a complete bar with a sink and an ice-making machine is concealed behind doors which have been treated in the same manner as the rest of the room. No attempt has been made to hide the television set, nestling among a rich display of books.
5/6. A coat cupboard, which was previously ungainly with its architrave and panels being so close to the corner of the wall and the stairs, is now virtually invisible when the door is shut.

1

2

5

6

☐ A series of different table lamps, all carefully related in texture, shape and colour to their immediate environment. In all cases they are an integral part of, though not slavishly matched to, the tablescape in which they stand.

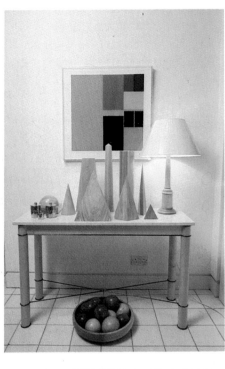 

Lamps and lighting

1. A parabolic adjustable spotlight is ideal for creating exciting pools of light and for focusing on pictures and objects.
2. A square recessed downlighter gives dramatic, functional lighting.
3. A brass desk lamp with a triangular shade is practical and stylish.
4. Uplighters can be finished in a variety of ways. This one has a bright bronze anodized finish and is operated by a foot switch.
5. Downlighters suspended on a light track can be swivelled in any direction and moved from left to right.

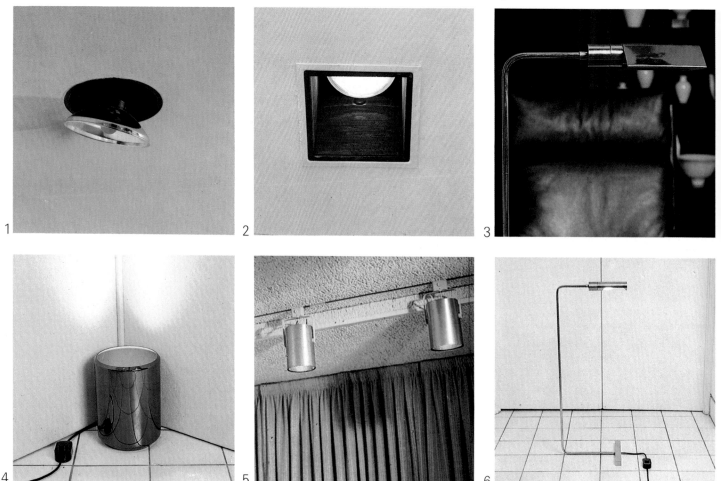

6. Elegant, thin-stemmed reading lights can look very good when placed on either side of a sofa.
7. Exterior lighting at night can be both dramatic and attractive. Here two spotlights are welcoming to visitors as well as being useful from a security point of view.
8. An eighteenth-century-style brass chandelier with partly recessed bulbs at the top of the metal candle tubes throws light on to the ceiling of this staircase hall.
9. A reproduction nineteenth-century kolser oil double lamp with green glass shades lights a collection of eighteenth-century boxes.

8

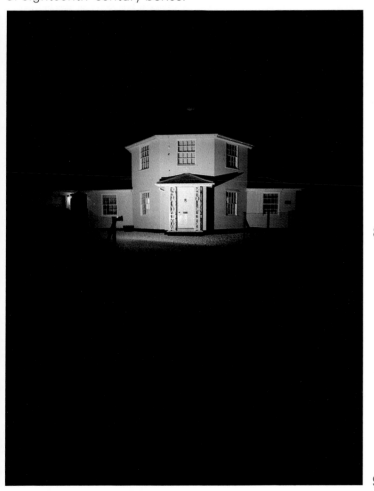

9

Dining-rooms

1. I designed an iron and stone sideboard for the dining-room of this seventeenth-century house in Holland. Rush matting covers the floor and the beamed ceiling is painted white.
2. A dining-room with green and white walls, stained wooden chairs and a natural wood table has a fresh, country appeal although it is in a suburban house.
3. In a Chelsea house the dining-room is at garden level. The room is a symphony of blues; chairs of

1

2

3

Queen Anne design have been lacquered with brilliant cornflower blue and the roman blinds are of fine blue-and-white percale. The circular table has a permanent cloth to the floor, with innumerable top-cloths and matching napkins which

□ Dining-rooms must always be serious. They can have good, exciting colour and pattern as long as it is fairly quiet. The most important point to consider in the room at night is the quality of light. To my mind, naked candles are an anathema; I like to use old-fashioned brass fitments holding opaque card shades which gently descend as the candle burns down. Good lighting is needed over the serving table and rather subdued light in the eating area, though you must be able to see your food. Sometimes I use parabolic spotlights directly above the dining table, but always on a rheostat switch so that the level of light can be varied.
□ Sideboards should be most carefully considered and I advocate a built-in hot-plate flush with the surface of the sideboard. The smell of cooking is unattractive when you enter a dining-room so I have designed small electric burners for burning essences which make the room smell fragrant.
□ Polished mahogany tables need a lot of maintenance so I invariably specify for clients a cheap block-board table with a tablecloth to the ground and washable top-cloths. Larger tops in two joinable sections for use when entertaining, which can be stored away, are practical. I like to have small decorative objects on a dining-room table, not just candlesticks and a vase of flowers. Snuffboxes for sweeteners or toothpicks and cigarette boxes look decorative, but I never put fruit on the table. It is important that a room where one sits as well as eats should, when not being used for eating, appear to be just a living-room; at such times I usually have a pile of books, a plant or a vase of flowers on the table.

can be laundered easily. The lithograph by Miró looks perfect on the complicated geometric walls.
4/5. A simple breakfast-room in an eighteenth-century country house. The scrubbed pine table and sideboard mix well with the green-

painted, rush-seated dining chairs. Some early eighteenth-century country pottery has been arranged on a series of plywood brackets. The pottery jars on the sideboard contain brown sugar, chutney and other country goodies.

4

5

Tour of the USA

☐ The United States is way ahead of every other country in the world in terms of interior design. Every single town has at least one interior decorator and large cities several hundred; some are exceptionally good. The problem at the moment is that interior design there has becomes very indigestible to me. Every magazine you open has pattern on pattern, thing on thing, influence on influence. There is little disciplined handwriting.
☐ But I must admit that I have

seen, over the years, more exciting and controlled decoration and interior design in New York, San Francisco, Chicago and Santa Barbara than in any other country. With the exception of two European cities, the interiors that have influenced me most were in those cities.
☐ It was therefore very flattering to me that I was asked to design carpets and fabrics for the US decorators' market and when I was asked in 1968 to design a range of

towels and sheets for a large American manufacturer I accepted the challenge with relish. When the collection was ready I went on a promotional tour of the United States, visiting twenty-one cities in two and a half weeks, travelling in the company jet. I lectured to audiences of five hundred at a time in department stores, visited their book departments which carried my latest publications, and the linen departments where in-store designers had devised room

settings based on my ideas, using my sheeting material for curtains or to cover improvised tester beds. I gave interviews to the press, radio and television, answered questions at the end of talks and gave individual consultations.

□ The whole tour was tremendous fun; the only disappointment was that I never had time to see any of the buildings or museums in those cities which I had not visited previously. It was rather like taking part in an election campaign – I

was up at 6.30 to be on time at a radio station or a television studio, then it was on to lecture at a store at 11.00, lunch with the president of the store and by 3 o'clock we were in the air again heading for the next city. At each airport three Cadillacs were always at the steps of the plane, one for us, one for the photographer, public relations officers and tour manager, and one for the luggage. We were whisked straight off to the hotel where the manager would take us up

to the roof-top presidential suite – my wife's favourite soap and our choice of soft and hard drinks would be already in place.

□ I have never found lecturing or speaking in public difficult, because, from a very early age, my mother made me participate in amateur theatricals and I was never allowed to appear unless I projected my voice properly. It was easy for me to perform in America. I was talking about a subject that I eat, sleep and drink – design.

☐ I am deeply interested in architecture of all periods. Architectural detail is design and design should be architectural. Architectural shapes such as the pyramid and obelisk occur a great deal in my work; perhaps this is because I was brought up in East Anglia, surrounded by all those spires on the wool town churches. The obelisk is a great feature of Egyptian architecture which I have always loved. It is tall and elegant; it has proportion and style. In fact obelisks are a recurring feature in almost every great period of building – Roman, Renaissance, baroque, neo-classical. In its rounded form the obelisk appears today in factory chimneys and power stations, which can be very beautiful. The column, whether it be Doric, Ionic or Corinthian, appears frequently in architecture of all periods. (I mention the orders in my order of preference.) Any designer who is architecturally orientated must love these elegant shapes.

☐ I have been involved in giving architectural advice throughout my career – starting with a garden pavilion for Mrs Douglas Fairbanks, small temples in Belgrave Square, houses in Switzerland, Australia and America and more recently at Barons Court, the library at Easton Neston, the new house at Syncombe Park, the remodelling of Gatcombe Park, the Octagon House and the new agricultural housing at Britwell. It is

important to remember, however, that interior
designers cannot be architects and that architects
cannot be interior designers. They should and can
work harmoniously together. There are few architects
who really understand eighteenth- and early
nineteenth-century thinking; I think I do because I
have lived with it for so long. It has always been one
of my passions – especially details such as doorways
and porches because they contain so many marvellous
variations.

□ I am equally passionate about modern architecture.
One of the most exciting moments in my life was
when I saw the Seagram building in New York for the
first time in 1956; today it holds just as much
excitement for me as that very first experience. The
opera house in Sydney is one of the greatest
architectural objects in the world, as is the
Guggenheim Museum, designed by Frank Lloyd
Wright. It should have been his mausoleum, however,
for it is awkward as a picture gallery. Modern
architecture has to be immaculate and well
maintained.

□ Internal architecture is a vital ingredient of good
interior design – whether it be period, where it
needs restoring or having later modifications removed,
or whether it is the interior of a new house or building.
Too little real consideration is given to good detailing.

Windows and curtains

1. In a recently completed house in New South Wales, the architect created for the bedroom a very interesting ceiling design which posed considerable problems for the curtain-maker. I designed these curtains which reef up in two great swags on either side of the windows, softening the vast areas of glass that were essential because of the spectacular view from the room. I painted the walls and ceiling and carpeted the floor in the same turquoise blue as the curtain fabric, and covered the beds and sofa in a similar blue printed on a white background.

2. A room before being furnished, showing the banded treatment on the walls with complementary inset bands on the dress curtains and roman shades. The colours are carefully co-ordinated with the carpet.

3. In order to control the daylight in the bedroom of an eighteenth-century country house, I used beige holland roller blinds for the windows. The curtains were made in the same material as that with which I draped the four-poster bed, whose pelmets were based on some from the late seventeenth century.

4. I particularly dislike curtains that go across walls between windows placed very near to each other. In this instance, in the library of a house in Sydney, I deliberately let the shiny yellow walls show between the curtain treatment. The pelmet is an elaborately shaped one, inspired by early nineteenth-century Eleutheran balustrade designs. The textured brown carpet relates to the brown trimming on the curtains and works pleasantly with the pale cerulean blue sofa.

5. A room setting created in an American department store, using one of my bed-linen designs for the

1

3

5

6

curtains, which are pleasantly co-ordinated with the upholstery on the sofa and armchair and the fur rug. Dark brown dominates the build-up of natural colours.

6. In this London room the curtains, with French headings, are lined on the leading edge with an inset band of dark aubergine which is picked up on the trimmings of two of the cushions in the room.

7. Faced with a small bedroom with unattractive metal window frames, I filled the room with a tester bed fixed directly on to the ceiling; I covered the bed on the exterior with yellow glazed chintz bound with orange, and on the interior with a small cotton print of my design. The window curtains of cream glazed chintz exactly match the walls. In the daytime the holland blind is always kept at the level shown here to hide the horizontal glazing bar two-thirds of the way up the window. Stainless steel grilles help even more to minimize the effects of the badly proportioned windows.

8. In a Brussels office I used roman shades, bound at the base and on the outside edges; they fit neatly into the window openings. The dark brown and off-white geometric carpet works well with the colours of the roman shades and linen-covered wall panels.

9. The same textured linen has been used to cover the wall panels and the roman shade in this detail; in contrast, the squab window cushion was made of a shiny plastic upholstery cloth.

10. In a London bedroom I used the same fabric, the colours of which are clearly co-ordinated with the carpet, for the curtains, the inside and outside of the tester bed, the fabric-wrapped writing desk and the low four-panelled screen.

11. For the vast Edwardian windows of my St Regis Hotel suite in New York I made curtains which were permanently joined at the top, and held back lower down by large tie-backs. At night they remained like this so that the dramatic view over New York would not be hidden. The mirrored screen gives a sense of height and glamour to the room, which I painted white to make the Edwardian feeling of the plasterwork recede.

12. I used roman shades for a reconstructed bay window in a Chelsea house, and in front of them I placed a Buddha's head behind two stacks of suede leather floor cushions.

8

9

11

12

Windows and curtains

□ Windows exist to be looked out of and to let in daylight. The illustrations here are of views from the windows at Britwell and show the importance of a simple, uncluttered frame to optimize the vista beyond.

□ The treatment of windows can totally alter the atmosphere of a room and the style of a house, and it is sad that nobody has been asked to design standard windows of eighteenth- and nineteenth-century style which could be mass-produced. It would help those unfortunate people now building new houses on a budget who are entirely restricted to what is currently available. It seems to me that there is a particular lack of well-designed, mass-produced windows of both traditional and modern design and also of bathroom units, light fittings, door handles, etcetera.

☐ A chevron design cut out in brown and white paper for one of my furnishing fabrics which was and still is very successful in America and England, forms part of a tablescape that also includes a fine bronze partly gilded Buddha. The gothic chair dates from about 1825, and the basket on the floor is filled with pot-pourri.

□ One of the many colour combinations in which the chevron design was printed.

☐ Curtains have two basic functions. The first is to keep out cold draughts in rooms where the windows are not double-glazed, and to enclose one at night. There are some instances, however, where I have hung curtains which I never intended to be drawn because the view by night is so exciting – for example, an apartment high up in a London block of flats or in a skyscraper in New York. The second function of curtains is to give a room a feeling of warmth and to frame the view attractively by day.

☐ One of the problems with windows in cities is that you do not want people to see in, but on the other hand you do want to be able to look out. Very little can be seen from outside, but if privacy is essential I always prefer to use horizontal or vertical venetian blinds rather than net, voile or lace curtains. If net curtains are used for this purpose they should have a very small repeat pattern and never be draped back.

☐ In many instances I prefer to use roman shades rather than curtains, particularly when I am aiming at a rather tailored interior such as one might want in an office. I also like to use festoon curtains which were used in the eighteenth century; they are simply reefed up on cords in great festoons and then let down at night like ordinary curtains.

☐ Curtains should usually go from the top of the window to the floor, because a curtain which ends at sill height looks very mean and awkward.

☐ Curtains, with the exception of those made from pure silk taffeta, hang much better if they are lined and interlined. I have often used dress fabrics for curtains – it can be less expensive but they do not always last as long. Sometimes I use dress curtains – these are ones which do not close – and then put a roman shade or laminated roller blind behind them. A contrasting band on the leading edge of a curtain can look well, as can inset bands of trimming.

☐ Shaped pelmets can be interesting and in a period room I often use swags, tails, ruching and bows.

☐ I believe in controlling daylight because the light is then more flattering to people in the room and to the room itself; I use festoon curtains, holland blinds or roman shades partly pulled down to achieve this.

☐ A roman shade in one of my geometric designs printed in white pigment on coarse beige cloth covers the lavatory window of an Australian house.

☐ An eighteenth-century gothic chair made for Horace Walpole and a mahogany candlestick holding a metal candle and card shade are dramatically silhouetted against an eighteenth-century window.

☐ The first foreign associate to open a shop bearing my name was Madame Fleur Vulliod in Switzerland. She wrote me a letter saying that she was devoted to my style, had a house near me in France and wanted to visit me. After I had talked to her for a couple of hours we decided that since she was using my ideas, my fabrics and worked in a very similar fashion to the way in which I worked, she should become my associate in Switzerland. I now have associates and shops in several other countries: Madame Barbara Wirth and Christian Badin in France; Nicole Cooremans in Belgium; Harry Horsburgh in Japan; Siegwart Pilati in Germany; Nigar Khan in Pakistan.

☐ All the shops are licence arrangements and my associates operate quite independently. I never look for associates – they always come to me first. They are already admirers of my style and they have my complete confidence. Sometimes a client wants to consult me personally, so I fly to Sydney, Tokyo, Antwerp or Geneva to give a first design brief and it may be a year or more before I return to see the finished result. I have never needed to alter any detailed design decision that has been taken by any of my associates.

☐ It is the co-ordination of colour in the objects, flowers, wallpapers and carpets, and the use of simple materials that has made my shops the success they are. The build-up of colours and the relationships between them give people a feeling of confidence.

1. The façade of my showroom in Jermyn Street.
2. The façade of David Hicks Belgium.
3. An internal skylight gives borrowed light to the staircase from the design studio of David Hicks Belgium. The red-painted window frame reflects the colour of the lamp.
4. Madame Cooremans and I designed the fitments on either side of the chimneypiece in the Brussels showroom specifically to take my carpet samples. The two scroll-top paintings are by Bruce Tippett.
5. A wood-panelled interior in one of the showrooms in David Hicks Belgium.
6. The build-up of colour is typical of my shops. Here various yellow objects relate to the lime green and yellow fabric on the armless chair and again to the pattern of the wallpaper on the panels hanging above the lamp.
7. Nicole Cooremans' office in David Hicks Belgium is painted white with white roller blinds banded with yellow at the base. The floor is covered in jute matting.

1

2

3

6

7

□ Early evidence of bed hangings appears in classical times and in medieval manuscripts. One of the best-known paintings which depicts them is *The Arnolfini Marriage* by Jan van Eyck, in which the bed hangings are pulled up into a balloon in one corner so that the artist can show us more of the interior of that delicious Flemish house. The hangings on these tester beds were very practical: they gave privacy and protection against the cold. They were only used by very grand people.

□ There are many different ways of developing the tester bed theme; the pelmet can be shaped in many different ways, and for inspiration I sometimes look at the copper or wooden pelmets around garden pavilions and balconies in city squares, on railway stations and, of course, in historical paintings of tester and canopy beds. The beds can be half-testers, coming out about two feet from the wall; they can also have domed tops which do not need poles to support them. The framework can be bolted to the ceiling. I have placed beds in the middle of a bedroom and attached the draperies to a corona on the ceiling. When I was touring America in 1968 I devised a very simple and inexpensive way of

1

making tester beds in order to display the materials that I had designed.

□ Bedspreads look well quilted. I like to cover the top side of eiderdowns in the same fabric as the bedspread, providing that it is not too thick – a heavy eiderdown is most uncomfortable. Headboards, which can be shaped or rectangular, are best loose-covered so that the cover can be cleaned. Bedroom lighting should be soothing and the lighting from bedside lamps should be controlled from the lamps themselves as well as at the door.

1. I fixed a pole high above this bed and draped over it a red, white and blue fabric lined with a similarly coloured cotton of a different pattern. To give a feeling of luxury I made an upholstered pad which I tied with ribbons to the headboard of the old Victorian brass bedstead. The walls are painted white and the floor is covered in white cord.

2. In a semi-circular-headed alcove I achieved a draped effect in a small-repeat red and green patterned cotton with an inset green and white floral border. The green of the bedside lamps is co-ordinated with the green of the fabric.

2

☐ I devised a shaped pelmet for this tester bed which I repeated over the curtains at the window. The walls were covered in yellow moiré as were the bed hangings, which were lined with yellow glazed chintz. The Hungarian needle-point carpet design from my collection was woven in pale green, yellow and faded apricot.

☐ In Paris with my associate I used a striped glazed chintz for the exterior of the *lit au baldoquin*, which is suspended from the ceiling, and for the curtains. It is romantic, feminine and very French.

☐ For my son's bedroom in our small London flat I devised a severe battlement-pelmeted tester bed and covered it in small brown on beige geometric print. I painted the walls beige and hung a series of prints on them.

☐ This four-poster is fixed directly to the ceiling in my London showroom and has an absolutely straight pelmet made of Etruscan red tweed, bordered with glazed chintz in a lacquer orange. The interior of the bed is in glazed raspberry pink chintz. The bedside tables are red perspex and hold red pottery lamps with white shades.

☐ We often display beds in my showrooms around the world and necessarily the accessories change from week to week.

☐ A small bedroom in a country house has yellow cotton stretched on the walls and covering the bed. The floor is close-covered in coconut matting in contrast to the armchair in polished brown leather. The curtains match the walls.

☐ For my daughters' bedroom in our London flat I made two shallow coronas with draperies in pink cotton and highly glazed yellow chintz trimmed with almond green velvet ribbon.

☐ An interesting treatment of the interior of a tester bed. Sun-ray pleating and inner and outer pelmets give an extra feeling of luxury.

☐ For the guest-room of a Sydney house I used beige linen with a white-pigment geometric print for the walls, curtains and draped bed, which was lined with white glazed chintz. I covered the floor in a brown and pale beige geometric carpet.

☐ A patterned fabric looks well for the exterior and interior of the double bed in this London hotel suite. The build-up of colour in the white-painted room was achieved through a mixture of pinks, reds and olive greens.

☐ Another view of the bed shown in the illustration on the left.

☐ A tester bed in my Paris showroom is covered on the outside in one of my geometric fabrics in yellow and pale peach and is lined with yellow glazed chintz. It stands on one of my bold geometric carpets in orange, peach, yellow and blue.

Beds and bedrooms

□ I make most of my tester beds on frames which are fixed directly to the ceiling. For the bed shown here (*right*) I used a plain green cotton for the exterior, and for the interior three differently patterned green and white Tarascon cottons redesigned from original *Directoire* blocks which I found in a factory in Provence. Looking straight up to the centre of the tester (*left*), the very fine sun-ray pleating makes a striking target effect. The bedspread (*centre*), base and headboard are covered in material of the same green and white but in a heavier design. I used this same fabric, picot-edged and ruched, and attached by two lines of stitching down the centre, to edge the valance and the bed curtains.

Wall treatments

☐ Wall treatments can alter a room architecturally and dramatically. Panelled effects can be achieved by using a striped border, painted on or with a narrow strip of striped wallpaper, or by using a braid or printed floral border stuck to the painted walls. Fabric-covered walls give a great sense of calm and luxury. The fabric can be stretched on batons and trimmed with braid or a self-covered band of buckram. Alternatively, blockboard panels can be fabric-wrapped and changed quite inexpensively after a few years – the material can be stapled on. Wallpaper can look deliciously fresh and can give great colour and style at quite a low cost.

☐ Dark, dramatic wall colours are more suited to a city apartment than a country house. I like to use lacquered wall treatments contrasting with matt-painted woodwork. It is always important to consider what the adjoining wall treatment will be – the inter-relationship matters very much.

1. This is a room for all seasons. Although the floated ceiling and basic walls are off-white, the panels of fabric contained within the red border can be changed to

suit the time of year. This is the summer scheme, with a grey, red and white theme. The sofa is covered in grey and white chintz, the wing chair in grey flannel suiting, and the low table in red tweed.

2. I used red fabric for the walls of this London living-room, and a red, beige and brown carpet of my own design which blends well with the mahogany table and antique chairs.

3. A large mural of Moscow makes an impressive wall treatment in the London sales office of the Russian national airline.

4. Objects often benefit from having a patterned wall behind them – in this instance a beige and white printed linen.

5. In a small cloakroom I created an unusual effect by covering the walls and table in the same paper.

6. In the Paris shop I used a red, green and blue wallpaper, the design of which I based on a nineteenth-century Turkish carpet.

7. Beige felt, with a contrasting blue braid, was used for the curtains, walls and day-bed upholstery in this town bedroom.

8. In a long corridor leading to an office reception area I used one of my patterned fabrics to cover the wall panel and a closely co-ordinated carpet for the floor.

9. I designed a damask fabric which I had printed in natural colours for the walls of a high-ceilinged Paris studio. They provide an excellent foil to the late seventeenth-century natural stone chimneypiece and the two fine Chinese lacquered screens.

10. For a fashion-fabric showroom I devised movable fabric-covered panels on which different examples of the merchandise could be displayed. I covered the armchairs in one of my client's overcoat materials.

☐ Walls of *faux granite*, which I achieved by stippling black paint with a sponge on a white background – one of the many decorative treatments employed on pine panelling in the early eighteenth century. The sad thing about this delightfully naïve way of painting rooms is that it was considered vulgar by the Victorians who almost inevitably painted it over. I first saw *faux granite* in the Pennsylvania Dutch Room in the Winterthur Museum near Wilmington, Delaware; other examples exist at Fawley Place, outside Henley, and at Great Hundridge Manor in Buckinghamshire.

Storage and display

1. A fine, mid-eighteenth-century writing desk holds a collection of eighteenth-century Chinese jade bottles, as well as books and magazines. On the writing surface are a number of objects and a watercolour of my father's carnations by my mother. The swan kolser oil-lamp has a green glass shade.
2. A gothic display cabinet, containing my mother's collection of china, is surmounted by an Edwardian *retour d'Egypte* clock, and is flanked by portraits.
3. A display fitment with glass shelves and a dark tweed background. The varied objects are lit dramatically with parabolic spotlights.
4. In a room with walls covered in green suede cloth I placed an obelisk of dark green perspex, in which to house icons and other

1

small objects.

5. A bookcase-table with a black lacquered finish and a black-and-white granite top. The black perspex pyramids contrast interestingly with the early Indian sculptured head. The mirror is framed in a boldly conceived moulding of pale sycamore.

6. Two bookcases, which I designed in the Egyptian manner, are made of mahogany with flush-inlaid ebonized details. There is a desk *en suite* and, talking to the desk, two honest-to-goodness brand-new chairs in the Regency style. The carpet was inspired by Navaho Indian weave designs. Two very neat triangular-section brass desk lamps give a totally practical but discreet light.

3

4

6

Storage and display

1. Although I do not like to use a lot of objects in libraries or on bookshelves, the occasional object or vitrine, such as the one shown here enclosing the five heads of Buddha, is acceptable to me.
2. A Romanesque earthenware figure of a woman, the colour of which combines well with the white vellum-bound books.

1

3. The colours in this lump of mineral reflect exactly those of the marbled endpapers of a book which once belonged to Sir Ernest Cassel, the Edwardian financier.
4. I am in the process of rebinding all the books in my library in scarlet, maroon and aubergine, with gold tooling.

Case history:
A Paris apartment

☐ For a Paris apartment which I redecorated with my associate, Christian Badin, we devised a complicated geometric inlaid marble floor for the entrance hall. Dramatic parabolic spotlights are focused on objects, trees and the floor.

☐ In the library, the fine *boulle* desk is successfully accompanied by a modern, leather-covered armchair. The room is lit with uplighters and brass reading lamps.

☐ Again in the entrance hall, the walls were lacquered in *sang de boeuf* so brilliant that it reflects the urns almost like mirror.

☐ In the dining-room we finished the mahogany *boiserie* in an eggshell polish, picking out the mouldings in white lacquer, and adapted it to take a fine eighteenth-century Chinese painted silk panel. Parabolic spotlights are grouped into circular shapes, while chandeliers, lit by real candles, hang above the two dining tables. The tablecloths are made of bold patchwork of contrasting pinks.

Furniture

□ I have been fascinated by furniture since I was ten years old. I bought my first antique chair in Sudbury when I was fifteen – a Regency chair with *faux* ebony and gilt decoration which I still have. I think I paid a pound for it.

□ Furniture, whether antique or modern, dictates the style which the interior design should be based, not on, but around. I have used, as people did in the past, old furniture in new interiors and new furniture in old houses. You often see seventeenth-century furniture in eighteenth-century houses working with great

1

2

3

style. I relish the use of Louis XV chairs in a modern interior and modern console tables in a fifteenth-century moated manor house.

□ I have designed a number of pieces of contemporary furniture but never a chair which was not traditionally inspired. Modern chairs are very difficult to design. The only really well-designed chair of the twentieth century is the one by Mies van der Rohe and that was done in 1929 – the year in which I was born.

1. A polished sycamore console table with a top surface of beige marble has thin bronze stretchers.
2. A modern commode, which I make with a shiny lacquer or eggshell lacquer finish. On this one the top is of honed stone.
3. I often cover the legs of tables and chairs in fabric. Here I have used one of my new geometric patterns on a straightforward modern armchair.
4/5/6. Two two-tiered perspex bedside tables of my own design, and a two-tiered plastic laminate one.

1. In this Paris apartment we used black-and-white fabrics of my own design for the roman shades (which cover the two openings on either side of the chimneypiece as well as the windows), the walls, sofa, chairs and even the mouldings of the chimneypiece. In contrast, the carpet is woven in three different reds which are repeated in some of the accessories such as the ashtray and cushions. The chandelier is fitted with real candles and hung rather low to make it more dramatic.

2. One of my Benson sofas covered in scarlet tweed is flanked by a pair of green lamps and two transparent obelisks housing some objects. On the floor is one of my patterned carpets in scarlet, blue and yellow.

3. Three distinct periods of European furniture mingle successfully in this London flat – two swan Empire chairs covered in red tweed are juxtaposed with Louis XVI polished walnut elbow chairs, George II gilt mirrors and George III eagle tables. It is because these pieces form such strong contrasts that they can live happily

1

2

3

next to each other. The tablecloth is embroidered Indian cotton and the carpet one of my Brussels weave designs.

4. My associate, Christian Badin, placed a Louis XV chair and a *Regence console* in a Paris bathroom, to contrast with the chromium and glass-shelved unit by the bath. I always like to see furniture and pictures in bathrooms if there is enough space and there nearly always is. On the walls is my Hungarian needlepoint wallpaper in pale blue, saffron and pink.

5. A small sitting-room has viridian green walls, a wall mirror to give a greater sense of space, elegant electrified candlesticks and an Indian cotton dhurrie on the floor. The bookcase and chair are covered in one of my small-patterned fabrics.

6. The library of my French associate, Madame Wirth, contains Louis XVI-style bookshelves, and a Louis XV leather armchair at a glass-topped writing table which holds, among other objects, an Egyptian-influenced mask by Robert Courtwright.

5

1. A traditional wing chair with an ebonized frame covered in black-and-white fabric with black piping.
2. A Victorian oak vestry chair given an updated feeling with a bright patchwork cushion.
3. A cane and chrome chair has a cool, fresh look.
4. A modern copy of a *Directoire* stool with a gold and white finish.
5. A polished wood *Directoire*-style chair upholstered in one of my geometric fabrics.

1

2

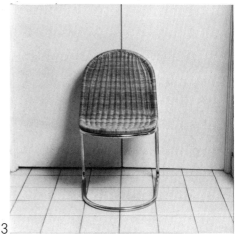

7

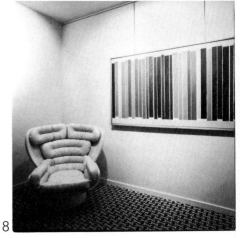

8

11

6. A Louis XVI-style *bergère* covered in black glazed chintz and finished with a double welt of the same material.
7. A day bed covered in ultra suede trimmed at the base with contrasting braid.
8. A white leather armchair designed by Colombo.
9. Grey and white glazed chintz on a sofa which is distinguished by the rather special knife-edge upholstery.

10. The reception area of a London office has concealed lighting behind a floated ceiling. The same striped material has been used for the sofa, curtains and wall panels.
11. An eighteenth-century French chair covered in brown horsehair with a white painted frame stands in front of a George II porphyry-topped side table.
12. In an Australian country house I used wicker chairs with simple white linen cushions; I put rush

matting on the floor and screened the windows with fine split-cane roller blinds.

5

6

10

Methods of working

□ At the first meeting with a new client in my London showroom I demonstrate various ideas at random to try to establish the kind of mood, the colour feeling, the style of furniture, the entertainment requirements and her likes and dislikes and those of her husband. The next stage is to produce coloured visuals in the studio with my assistants. Then my chief administrator, Susan Stafford, and chief interior designer, Paul Hull, produce the estimate and send out contractual letters, checking everything against the sample boards. Finally the visuals, sample boards and estimates are presented to the client in the office.

☐ My life has now become so highly organized that I have become a kind of design computer. Facts have been fed into me during the last twenty-five years, so that now any member of my organization, whether it be the chief product designer, Simon Thorpe, chief interior designer, Paul Hull, or an assistant in the shop, can simply come into my office and fire questions at me which I am able, through experience, to answer immediately. I may have initiated a scheme some weeks before which has then been adapted or modified to the client's own wishes, but perhaps there is one final question: 'What colour should those two chairs in the corner be?' I can certainly answer that quickly, but I can also answer other more complex problems with great speed.

☐ This might give the impression that work has become a bore or that everything is too easy: absolutely the reverse. It is still just as interesting, perhaps even more so, than a quarter of a century ago. I love dealing with the minutae of a situation when I am needed to do so, and have a firm grasp of what the situation artistically and financially involves.

☐ I do not find that my creativity is reduced by being at the head of an organization. Although I am always kept in the picture about day-to-day design decisions, I do not actually handle them myself for I have a very good team of assistants. But they can become too engrossed in down-to-earth details, while I am able to offer creative solutions of real help because I can take a bird's eye view.

☐ I always tell people when they first come to work for me that I do not want them to think, I do not want them to contribute, I want them simply to do what they are told. If they think that they have a positive contribution to make, they must not slow down the day's work by interrupting me then, but they are always free to come and have a drink with me that evening away from the office and say, 'Actually, why did you make that decision this morning?' or, 'Have you ever thought of doing it this way?' Provided creative employees are given that possibility, I find that they understand.

☐ Perhaps it is because I have strong views, I have published a number of books, made many statements and am rather a strong personality, that my employees know where they are and would not have come to work for me unless they admired my taste and style. We are sought by our manufacturers and customers because of our house style, because of our way of looking at things, because of our way of thinking; the longer I am in practice the more people naturally come to me because they know I am an expert in my field. I think that the creative people in my design teams all over the world are aware of that, and they know that their job is to give the Hicks solution.

☐ I am sometimes influenced by my staff, and a number of people who work with me have an interesting personal colour sense which, although not very different from mine, has its own character. I like to incorporate this into jobs we do because it gives a wider dimension to my colour thinking. Usually it will be a colour scheme which has been thought up in my absence; I may like it very much but I will probably change one thing, not just for the sake of making myself indispensable, but because often, good though the colour scheme may be, it may be impractical or lacking that spark or flair for which I have a certain reputation and which is what my clients want.

☐ I rarely take on people who have worked for other designers. Mostly they come straight from art school,

but schools can only teach theory.
□ My solutions to design problems
are usually inspirational because I
was not brought up at a drawing
board. On the other hand, my chief
interior designer, Paul Hull, thinks
best at a drawing board, as do my
other creative designers. When we
were working, for example, on two
restaurants in Japan, I said what
sort of atmosphere I wanted and
drew a few sketches, and they went
to their drawing boards, got out the
plans and worked from them. This
method gives me a lot of freedom in
thinking about design innovations.
□ As another example, I went to
Paris recently to see my associate
Madame Barbara Wirth's new Louis
XVI flat in the Place du Palais
Bourbon. Although it was empty, it
was absolutely charming. I saw
immediately how she could get
daylight into her husband's
dressing-room which had no
windows; I suggested two *oeil de
boeuf* windows, not horizontal but
vertical, on either side of a great
draped bed – one window was to
be real and the other a dummy: it
would be both attractive and
practical. She had not thought of
this and was thrilled.
Right A three-dimensional sketch
of my new drawing-room in the
country – a useful way of seeing
how the room will work.

Methods of working

□ A series of drawings, collages
and models which are the starting
point for contract interior schemes.
These are produced in my studio for
presentation to clients and also
serve as an *aide mémoire* as the
project progresses. We rarely
produce them for private jobs.

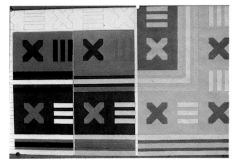

Doors and screens

Front doors give an instant initial impression of your life-style. If you are replacing a later front door in an old house, you can do no better than look at good, elegant designs of other period houses. Doors are a very important aspect of any room but they must open the right way, not immediately showing the bed or the lavatory. You can reverse the hanging of a door very easily.

□ One way to give height and proportion to a low-ceilinged room, if it has ordinary standard doors, is to put in tall doors going right up to the ceiling. When I did this in my old London flat, which was a miserable series of little boxes, it acquired enormous style and elegance and even tall people felt that it was a comfortable space in which to move, simply on account of the proportion of the doors.

□ Screens, whether real or false, have magic and give great atmosphere. They can be usefully employed to hide things, to contain things and to perform tricks. I have used them to house a wardrobe where I have not actually wanted a piece of furniture or when a piece of furniture has not been available, and I have used them when two doors were too close to each other. To conceal night storage heaters and radiators I often favo screens rather than radiator covers. I make them three feet high like the Louis XVI screens and they look very stylish.

1. In the dining-room of a house in Australia there was an awkwardly placed door leading to the kitchen. To conceal it, I fixed an eighteenth-century Chinese screen to both the wall and the door. A large *Ficus lyrata* towers to the ceiling, lit by an uplighter.
2. A series of doors in a country house in Ireland. All the doors and architraves have been stripped of paint and polished to reveal the warmth of the original 1870 pitch pine.

3. Some clients with a country house in New South Wales wanted to feature their collection of coloured glass in the entrance doorway to the house. With their architect, Richard Rowe, I devised a panelled door in limed oak, and made a surround of clear plate glass with glass shelves to hold the objects.

1. When I redesigned the internal architecture of two London flats, I re-formed the front doors which previously had been suburban-looking with dismal fanlights above them. I made the flush doors virtually from floor to ceiling, and added some good-looking door furniture. I curtained the stairs to hide an extremely ugly open lift-well, and used two downlighters to make the landing more interesting.
2. In the same London flat with four small rooms I punched openings through to the right and left of the four rooms and, at all four ends, introduced built-in cupboards with mirrors which gave an endless series of reflections.
3. Lack of space meant that the doors to this bedroom had to slide; to give them a greater sense of height, I made them floor-to-ceiling.

5

4. In a minute bathroom I placed the bath centrally along one wall. White-painted wooden screens at both ends gave the bath importance while retaining a sense of space. To the left of the bath I placed the lavatory, and to the right the washbasin, behind which the wall was mirrored above and curtained below.
5. For a room with no daylight I created an opening with a painted wooden grille, which made a good background for a fine early Indian wood carving. The room is enlivened by a series of blues – in wool, chintz, silk, lacquer, ceramic and scagliola lapis lazuli.
6. To give importance to a room in a rather plain thirties house in Chelsea, I created large, almost ceiling-height doors in dark rosewood and continued the wood in the skirting below the fabric-covered walls.

143

□ Office design could be considered boring compared with the design of domestic interiors, but I find quite the reverse is true because it presents the greatest possible challenge. It has been a very neglected field in the past but now it is fairly common practice to get professional interior design advice when a company either refurbishes their building or moves to a new one. Most of the offices which I visit are incredibly ill-organized, boring and ugly. I welcome the chance to re-design the offices of people who have to spend many hours of their lives in these areas. I improve their surroundings by giving them interesting patterned carpets, good practical lighting and colour. The style, colour, lighting and furniture layout can make a vast difference to the congeniality of an area or room in which office workers from the top to the most junior have to work. The great problem is always the personalia with which people will insist on surrounding themselves. Offices should be stark

□ For my London office I designed this plastic laminate desk which can serve as a conference table, a drawing table and a conventional desk. Two parts of the top open for correspondence, 'in' and 'out', while the other two sections contain drawers. Although the table does not take up much space, four people can have an extremely comfortable seated discussion.

and devoid of travel momentos, family photographs and outdated pipes : the atmosphere should be workmanlike and edited.

□ Occasionally a managing director will wholeheartedly support a scheme which I suggest but which does not appeal to other executives in the company. I have known instances where the executives have been positively unhappy with a spectacular colour scheme, perhaps involving lighting which they are not used to and unusual colours. Yet after two months in their new environment they have grown not only to like it, but to feel very proud of it. In fact it often happens that I propose something to a client and the client is not totally convinced of its suitability. But because I hold a certain professional standing the client finally accepts it. I am inclined to push people into agreeing to certain schemes if I myself believe that they are the right solution in a particular situation.

□ A small conference room has white-painted wooden screens covering the radiators, patterned velvet-upholstered chairs modelled on eighteenth-century originals, and a hexagonal table made of plastic laminate with an inset band of green.

Offices

1. A neutral off-white background in my London office enables me to use all kinds of different furniture from my showroom whenever I wish to promote it – in this case traditional dining chairs covered in red tweed. The floor is black parquet with the boards laid in diamond fashion fanning out from the centre. I used a red cord carpet with a black border. The walls are totally bare except for a single charcoal drawing by Bruce Tippett. The view from the window is uninspiring, so I screened both it and the radiator.

1

2

146

2. Two executives can work happily side by side at this desk without having to look at each other; a third sprig is for chairs for occasional visitors.
3. A conference room for junior executives is treated here in the simplest possible way, allowing them maximum concentration.
4. A dining-room in the London office of an Agent General has blue fabric-covered walls and moss green upholstered dining chairs.

3

4

1. To create a friendly, relaxed conference room as requested by a company I used a bold beige and scarlet carpet, covered the walls with beige striped tweed, and made a warm drinks area in red lacquer with embossed fitments.

2. I designed the London office of the managing director of an American film company entirely around his collection of antique chessmen which are displayed in the vitrine on the right. This photograph of the room at night, with curtains drawn, shows the dramatic ceiling downlighting which I used. Offices should always be well lit because businessmen often work quite late into the evening.

1

3. The managing director's office on the thirty-sixth floor of a building in New York. Because of the breathtaking view over Central Park the curtains are not intended to be drawn. The colour scheme is based on very dark brown men's flannel suiting on the walls, a brown, black and white geometric carpet, and geometric covers for the upholstered furniture. A glass trestle table is ideal for the top executive since all his files and papers are housed in his personal assistant's office next door.

☐ To compensate for the lack of natural daylight in this reception area I decided to use warm orange colours for the carpet, upholstery and fabric-covered walls. Large sofas give the room an expensive, comfortable feeling, reminding one more of a living-room than an office building.

☐ In the office of a merchant bank in the City of London the company logo was incorporated into the pattern of the carpet. The furniture is covered in dark grey tweed.

☐ A projection area forms part of the waiting-room in a sales office, the entire interior of which we remodelled.

☐ For a fashion and fabric showroom I devised movable fabric-covered panels on which the finished merchandise could be displayed. Two armchairs were covered in one of the company's overcoat materials.

☐ The reading area of a government office has black brick walls, timber-clad columns, and comfortable furniture covered in a practical dark brown tweed.

☐ In an open-plan office working areas are defined by smoked-glass, chromium-framed movable panels.

□ In a London bank I used a false ceiling, marble for the cash desk fronts and floor, and polished mahogany for the doors and counters.

□ Rich earth colours and plants in a city office help to relieve the strain of urban life.

□ Dark aubergine walls with scarlet detailing, a black egg-crate ceiling, stainless-steel chairs and black tables together create a dramatic atmosphere in a London shoe shop.

□ An executive office in London has a brown and beige patterned carpet, beige tweed-panelled walls with matching curtains and, at one end of the room, a blue sofa.

□ White plastic laminate units give the inhabitants of this open-plan office a degree of privacy.

□ In the executive office of a fashion house the pattern in the geometric carpet is entirely composed of the letter A, standing for the designer's name. The whole scheme is in black and white with the exception of the mahogany Louis XVI bureau.

☐ In my London headquarters, the office of my
managing director is next to that of the financial
director. The walls of both rooms have dark blue
fabric-covered panels, in the one case on a pale
emerald green wall surface, in the other on a scarlet
background. Both have ceilings and window screens
lacquered in dark blue, a geometric carpet of my own
design in the same dark blue, and steel-framed chairs.

1. The reception area for a large international company headquarters has tweed-clad wall panels framed in aluminium, scarlet-lacquered lift doors and an unusually shaped stainless-steel reception desk which conceals all the controls, such as closed-circuit television, intercom and telephones, from the public's gaze. The extremely strong geometric patterned carpet was inspired by a mosaic floor in St Mark's Cathedral in Venice. The company wanted a very forceful, exciting atmosphere which would enhance their product.
2. Rust-coloured tweed panels, roman shades with a black banded trim and brilliant yellow upholstery

create a warm atmosphere in another area of the same London sales office.
3. The receptionist's desk in this office is in blond sycamore inlaid with bronze panels; its high front and sides conceal a typewriter and telephones. In front of the desk is a Gainsborough chair covered in blue wool to match the walls.
4. For a New York company I devised a dramatic reception area with flush ceiling lighting to cast a cool light on the practical, patterned carpet. All the seating was upholstered in signal red and the walls were covered with grey flannel.

5. For a Commonwealth office I designed a reception desk with a top of marble from the country concerned, with panels of chamois leather framed in bronze. Dramatic spotlighting, a large dried flower arrangement and panels of burnt orange tweed reaching almost to the ceiling give the entrance an unbureaucratic look.
6. I made this striking black-and-white glazed tile design for the floor of a Park Lane property company, and placed an interesting bank of downlighters over the reception desk.

3

6

Case history:
A castle in Ireland

☐ In this bedroom in an Irish castle I used one of my
latest cotton prints for the curtains and pelmet,
together with a white holland roller blind. Since the
room faces south over an Atlantic bay I painted the
walls a brilliant sunflower yellow; I used yellow tweed
for the upholstery and yellow bedside lamps on either
side of the sugar-pink quilted bed.

□ I lit the drawing-room with uplighters placed behind the sofas and table lamps in off-white and orange. Sofas covered in orange, tan and fig red tweed relate in an interesting way to the aubergine, white and orange geometric carpet. The two early Georgian chairs are covered in white tweed.

Case history:
A castle in Ireland

☐ An awkwardly shaped Victorian bedroom seemed to me to need an overwhelming bed, so I designed one which hangs from the ceiling. I covered it on the outside with plain green cotton trimmed with a patterned green frill, and on the inside with green and white cotton – all the greens working happily together. On the walls is a pale green, pink and cream paper and the carpet, woven in my Celtic design inspired by the Book of Kells, also contributes to a green-on-green colour scheme.

☐ The dressing table is covered in a green and white geometric design and holds an Edwardian Sheraton dressing mirror and two vases of wild flowers.

□ The bathroom and dressing-room can be seen beyond, both continuing the green colour scheme.

□ A 1930s' portrait of Lady Mountbatten hangs over a simple bow-fronted chest of drawers, on which are a lacemaker's lamp, an Indian stone head and some arum lilies.

Case history:
A castle in Ireland

☐ Pink and white wallpaper and deep pink patterned cotton curtains and bedspread create a cosy Victorian interior in a tower bedroom.

☐ William Morris wallpapers had originally been used in the castle, and I reprinted his design for the study, which has pitch-pine window frames and shutters, a geometric carpet and wool curtains. The photograph shows the room at night, with the curtains open, when the view is particularly attractive with twinkling lights in the far distance.

☐ For the entrance hall, staircase and first-floor landing I reprinted another Morris wallpaper in mid-brown and white, which works well with the stone capitals of the 1874 gothic internal architecture and the beige cord matting on the floor. I left the stone-framed windows uncurtained. A portrait by Derek Hill of Lord Mountbatten hangs half-way up the second flight of steps.

☐ I take great delight in architectural detail and when I am creating the internal architecture of a room I take my inspiration from the past unless the room is modern in style. When working in a historic house I always take great care to specify exactly the way that plasterwork, mouldings, architraves, window surrounds and ceilings should be decorated.

☐ I often find one part of an elaborate entablature which could be used to great advantage on its own in a simpler situation.

Mouldings

1. I love carved and moulded models of animals. Here a French cast-iron retriever puppy, painted beige, sits disdainfully on a front doorstep.
2. A shell-topped niche in an eighteenth-century entrance hall contains a reconstituted stone urn on a block of antique marble.
3. A detail of an English baroque stone chimney is topped with a contemporary plaster vase of flowers.
4. A chimneypiece dating from about 1760 in carved, white-painted wood with white marble slips is handsomely shown off by walls covered in buttermilk and white woven cotton.

1

3

4

☐ I have had a sense of collections, however small and simple, ever since I was a child. I am an inveterate buyer and collector, not necessarily of valuable pieces, but of objects which have got some particular interest for me. It might be texture, or colour, or period which appeals; perhaps just a fragment of an eighteenth-century roof tile from China, or a piece of an Egyptian basalt hawk's head – not the kind of thing which would cost thousands of pounds at auction but something you can buy quite reasonably if you search.

☐ I first became aware of the importance of the relationship of objects when visiting museums and looking at their showcases. The first tablescape that I saw in a private house was in the home of Roderick Cameron, a collector of extremely varied possessions, the second in the home of Winifreda, Countess of Portarlington. Both these friends had a very strong influence on my taste in the fifties. Each of them, in his or her own very particular way, had a marvellous sense of relating one object to another, a group of objects to a picture, a picture to some objects and plants, the lamp, the light-fitting or the filtered daylight to the whole ensemble, and then all of this was related to the groups of seating. In their houses one always found a piece of furniture 'talking' to another – two chairs 'talking' to a sofa for instance. Even if there was no one in the room you could imagine the ease and comfort with which people could be seated in conversation with one another: the light was right, the room smelt right, and the objects had affinity.

☐ It is perhaps I who have made tablescapes – objects arranged as landscapes on a horizontal surface – into an art form; indeed, I invented the word. But I owe so much to these friends and to another legendary man of taste, Wright Luddington. What is important is not how valuable or inexpensive your objects are, but the care and feeling with which you arrange them. I once bought six inexpensive tin mugs in Ireland and arranged them on a chimneypiece to create an interesting effect in a room which otherwise lacked objects. They stood there in simple perfection.

☐ A group of objects of vaguely similar texture, colour and character is far more effective than just one piece. I took some simple small pebbles which I picked up on the Acropolis: one on its own would mean nothing but related to each other in an enamel saucer they became a fascinating little stonescape. I put next to them a small porphyry Egyptian snake's head, a circular porphyry box and another circular box in black-and-white granite. There was a relationship between them which worked.

☐ I never have time to spend a day looking for objects but passing through a store in a foreign country, driving past a shop in London or looking at an advertisement, I will suddenly see something I like, although I would only buy an object on its own knowing that I was going to get others to go with it. When I am on holiday in the Bahamas I often collect shells on the beach with the children and then we sort them into colours. As a result I have three pottery containers filled with different coloured seashells; they are perfectly valueless but they are attractive and have style. I have never despised simple things.

☐ I have been into far too many rooms in good houses where the furniture has been well chosen and the carpets and curtains have been suitable, but the whole effect is let down by a miserable little Meissen china lady and two silver geegews on a huge surface. It is better to have nothing at all than to have the wrong objects juxtaposed. The scale of objects in relation to table tops and other surfaces like chimneypieces is important – it is another of the areas where people go frightfully wrong. They do not think, they have no sense of scale, and they do not spend enough money on a large enough object in the first place.

☐ I once had drinks with Philippe de Rothschild's wife, before she was married, in a room which was absolutely stark. It had a parquet floor, beautiful French panelling on the walls, a pile of cushions and, in the corner, a galvanized iron bucket absolutely full of white lilies. This impressed me enormously; she had rejected the idea of having even a sofa until she could get exactly the sofa she wanted. All she nêeded was something soft on which to sit or lie, and flowers – because she felt passionately about flowers. This to my mind sums up the whole principle of rejecting everything until you find what you want.

☐ As far as my clients go, I would rather they found their own objects because this is one personal contribution which they can make. However, one of the great sadnesses about working for people who are well-off is that I may create a marvellous background, and perhaps they already have some good pictures – they might even ask my advice about buying some good furniture – but they always seem to fall down over objects. They do not seem aware of the need for good small things although fabulous ones are available in London, Paris and New York. A real feeling for objects is a very rare thing.

1. Pencils massed in a container both look decorative and are useful, but they must all be the same colour and be sharpened. Behind the pencils, a simple pottery bowl holds sandalwood sawdust which I brought back from India.

2. Shooting-sticks, umbrellas, parasols from Bali and flywhisks have been massed in a nineteenth-century cast-iron walking-stick stand to make an interesting group.

3. A nineteenth-century horn beaker holds a number of pipe cleaners which I think are very decorative, as well as being useful.

4. On a metal-framed, glass-topped table I placed a glass ashtray and glass cigarette box. In the background a piece of Persian jewellery hangs from a modern metal frame, while in a glass case I displayed a Mogul jewel.

5. On a Louis XVI *bonheur du jour* I placed a number of pieces of eighteenth-century pewter in front of a modern French painting. It makes an unlikely but interesting combination.

6. A collection of gilt boxes grouped under a white lamp with pale pink geraniums.

7. On a circular table with a cloth from Bali I have placed three wooden bowls containing seashells collected by my children and sorted into colours. Bursting out of a square pottery vase is an Indian sandalwood garland.

1

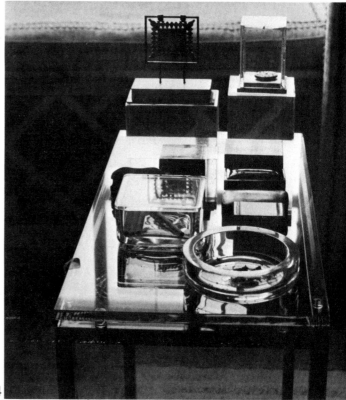

4

3

7

1

2

4

5

3

6

1. In a bedroom of a house designed by Sir John Soane I used some Victorian gilt brackets to hold a collection of blue-and-white vases, and hung four early nineteenth-century watercolours of Indian river scenes.

2. I placed this early nineteenth-century side table with a marble top in front of a false door in a rotunda. Bronze Regency vases were converted into lamps. The clock was too small, so I made it a simple, white-painted base to improve its proportions in relation to the room.

3. Three star-framed portraits make an interesting arrangement between the candelabra.

4. In the long gallery of a classical house I placed a large book-table with a settee on either side, one looking through a vista of rooms, the other out through French windows to distant hills.

5. An opaque white shade and picture lights produce warm and subtle lighting for the paintings and objects in this group.

6. A large marble vase on an ochre-coloured scagliola base makes a pleasing juxtaposition with the Restoration portrait on an easel.

1

2

3

□ It is extraordinary how interesting an effect can be created by grouping together the simplest of objects. On the raw plaster walls of my garden room at Britwell I fixed two plywood panels to hold various carved wood and plaster details.

1. The two caryatids are Jacobean oak. When I found them they were almost black, but I left them in a bath of bleach for some days and they emerged a beautiful colour.

2. This wallscape includes some balustrades from an early nineteenth-century house on Eleuthera in the Bahamas; they have much in common with nineteenth-century station canopy details. I often get inspiration from these shapes when designing pelmets for curtains or modern banisters. I love the colour of the bleached wood which still has traces of gaudy paint from long ago.

3. The gothic carvings are mid-nineteenth-century and probably came from a church screen. To the right is a corner detail from an Irish Regency house which is now in ruins; and below, the white-lacquered plywood panel with concentric circles was a prototype for a client's bathroom cupboards in the sixties.

4/5/6. In another corner of the room I have massed a collection of widely differing objects on a simple iron *étagère*. On the top shelf an eighteenth-century cast-iron urn towers above other finials. The central one was originally on top of the roof of an early nineteenth-century Eleutheran house and is a crude attempt to represent a pineapple – pineapple-growing being the island's main industry at that period. The ball next to it comes off a laundry post, and the pine ball on the right is brand new. On the two lower shelves are a collection of birds' nests found by my children, the top of a nineteenth-century stone urn and, at the base, a piece of driftwood found on the Isle of Wight.

Objects and tablescapes

1. A pottery camel by Marie Gill is placed on a table with a huge arrangement of dried hydrangea blossom.
2. A model of my house in the country made for my children out of thirty building bricks. It is not perfect architecturally, although the window sizes and general proportions are correct. It is a confusing thing to reassemble, the problem being that in a classical house the front and back elevations, the central bay windows and corner blocks are all almost identical.

1

2

3

4

5

6

3. An obeliskscape in front of architectural drawings and an engraving of three obelisks.
4/5/6. Marvellous architectural details can sometimes be found on demolition sites and bought comparatively cheaply from the firm concerned.
7. A simple basket containing hard, shiny spheres with opaline and lustre glazes.
8. Two paper-thin jade Mogul cups and saucers are mounted on clear perspex cubes of different heights to give added interest, and housed under perspex covers for safety.
9. A triangular table is covered in a quilted orange glazed chintz cloth producing an interesting multiple of triangles. A black perspex pyramid with two orange balls and two lacquer boxes make up this tablescape.
10. A wooden apple, banana and two pears would mean little individually, but grouped together on a red-lacquered table top they look effective.

8

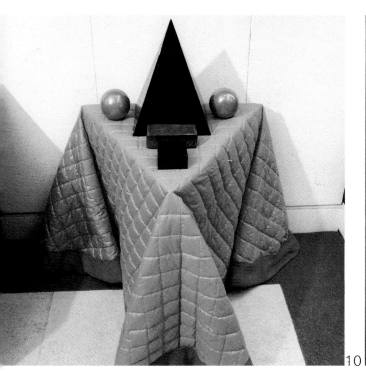

10

177

□ On this page I have arranged the same eleven objects in a number of variations to illustrate how simply one can alter the mood, emphasis and interest of a tablescape.

  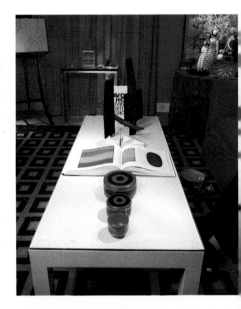

179

Objects and tablescapes

1. An Indian bust subtly lit from a semi-circle of polished brass which is almost lost among the smaller objects grouped on the red table top.

2. Inexpensive objects related by colour can be grouped together to achieve the maximum effect. The objects here are in different shades of aquamarine blue, reflecting the blue of the watercolours by Nigel Hughes above them.

3. An autumnal room setting in my London shop. Three dramatic paintings by Rib Bloomfield hang over an aubergine sofa massed with brilliant orange, yellow and violet cushions. The table holds some modern pottery, triangular perspex boxes, an antique plate and some

primitive African necklaces made of traders' beads. Although I would rarely use such violent colours in a client's house, individual ingredients from the group would look well in a simple modern setting.

4. A basket of glazed pottery balls and a number of other small objects make an interesting arrangement on a red fabric-covered table.

5. An early Georgian table holds a variety of unusual and unexpected objects: a series of baskets from around the world; a carved Egyptian mummy's head from a sarcophagus, standing on an orange perspex cube; a feather duster, from a Pacific island, which gives texture and life to its corner of

1

2

3

5

6

the table. The painting is by
Andrew Yates.
6. Two tablescapes, totally
unrelated, but working happily
together. The farther one contains
some yellow Chinese objects and a
gilded figurehead from an
eighteenth-century barge, which
are housed on a snakeskin-covered
table of my own design. An abstract
painting by Peter Upwood, an
Australian artist, hangs above the
group. On the marble-topped
French metal table is a collection of
blue objects in glass and lapis lazuli;
individually they are of little
interest, but grouped together they
make an effective tablescape.
7. Yellow and red marbled tulips
nestle in a tablescape of beige and

terracotta objects of widely
differing dates; a standing figure
from Sierra Leone has in front of it a
pre-dynastic Egyptian vessel; on
the right, a terracotta and white
glazed pot thrown by my nephew is
backed by a gilded Mogul dagger;
peering through the tulips is a pre-
Christian mask from Byblos. Over
the tablescape hangs an abstract
painting by Robert van Eyck.
8. A tablescape containing a head
and torso from Thailand on a
porphyry scagliola-topped table
with an ebonized base which I
designed. A painting by Sandra
Blow hangs on beige, felt-covered
panels in a recess of a white-
walled, white-tiled room.

4

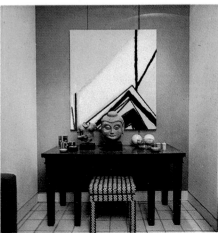

8

☐ I used to stay in a suite which I designed and which bore my name in the St Regis Hotel in New York whenever I was in that city – about seven times a year. The redecoration of the suite was part of the promotion campaign by the American manufacturers who had commissioned me to design a range of sheets and towels and it involved using these designs. Colonel Astor, who built the hotel in 1900, had a great deal of French furniture made at the time which was of superb quality with no pretension to being antique. I enjoyed mixing my designs with the original furniture and it made a very interesting ambience.

Restaurants and hotels

□ I have designed over twenty restaurants, each with a totally different atmosphere. They range from my first, the Gay Gordons in Glasgow, all tartan and brass chandeliers, to the Grange in Covent Garden, with tapestry walls and seventeenth-century detail; from one in Chelsea which was all blue and white to another in the same area with orange walls and purple upholstery.

1

1/2. For a western-style restaurant on the fiftieth floor of a newly built Tokyo tower block I designed all the internal architecture, furniture and fitments – including the chandeliers. Large structural beams dictated a ceiling solution of floating gilded panels against a black background containing a generous quantity of parabolic spotlights which are trained on to individual tables.

2

3. Chinese food is popular in Japan and this photograph shows a Chinese restaurant which I designed in the same building. I used a similar solution for the ceiling but made it more elaborate by adding flower motifs which stand out in relief. Chinese fretwork, scarlet-lacquered screens and Chinese Chippendale chairs give the room an oriental flavour.

1/2. The dining-room and bar of a motel outside London are related by having the same patterned carpet. Roman shades, curtains and wooden grilles all help to give character to an otherwise plain modern building. The budget was rather tight and the chairs were the best-looking ones I could find within the price range, but by covering them in brilliant red tweed I made them look more exciting.

3/4. I created the internal architecture of this London restaurant out of a disused warehouse. I featured the beams, which were already there, by painting them brown and faded vermilion. The floor is salami-coloured terrazzo divided into squares with ebonized

1

2

3

4

wood. The modern chandeliers and the frames of the nineteenth-century Dutch portraits are made of stainless steel and were designed specially for the restaurant. The bar, which can be seen in the distance, was inspired by the Carolean pews in Rycote Chapel, in Oxfordshire. In a further section of the restaurant (4) I covered the walls in one of my Brussels-weave carpets, creating a tapestry effect.

5/6/7/8. The problem of designing a restaurant is to think up a theme which is original but at the same time warm and inviting. For a London restaurant with very little daylight I decided to use a fresh blue-and-white colour scheme: the tablecloths, chairs, curtains, napkins, even the fabric on the walls, are all different blue-and-white cottons from the David Hicks France range. The inexpensive blue-and-white plates form interesting geometric patterns on the walls, lit by parabolic spotlights on the ceiling. Individual low-voltage chromium-finished table lamps light the food and tablecloth, and reflect a flattering light on to the diners' faces from below. For one wall (8) I created a gardening trophy out of ordinary garden tools which I sprayed white, giving the effect of eighteenth-century plasterwork. The chandelier is made of highly polished chrome in the Dutch style.

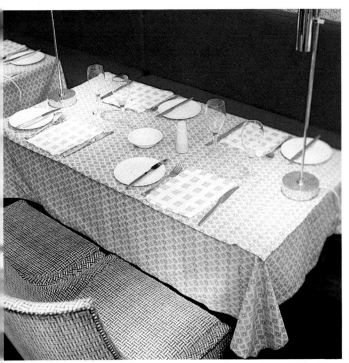

6

8

Shops

□ The fault of most shops is that they do not have enough atmosphere. I create atmosphere by the use of strong dramatic colours and extremely carefully thought-out lighting. Where an accessory is needed, I try to make it as unlike a piece of commercial furniture as possible, even though it may be quite inexpensive. I have always aimed at giving a strong feeling of interior design, as opposed to that of shop-fitting designers, whenever I have designed a shop. Every aspect – the

□ Two showrooms for a London shoe company where I was confronted with a newly constructed building and was therefore able to devise the internal architecture exactly as I wanted. It seemed to me important to create an extremely simple, plain background because the merchandise was small in scale. Dark, soothing colours allied with subtle indirect lighting are good elements for sales areas. In order to make the atmosphere reasonably uncommercial I used deep-buttoned leather sofas and modern, tweed-covered fitting chairs, with the occasional table lamp.

shop front, writing paper, carrier bags, wrapping ribbon, offices, delivery van – need vary careful consideration to achieve a successful result. Both shops and showrooms benefit from a strong sense of design, fitness of purpose and style, allied with good lighting.

❏ I have designed a number of shops for my licence operations abroad in association with my local associates. I find it intriguing that, although all the David Hicks shops sell more or less the same merchandise, each one has a totally different atmosphere and flavour which has been created by the taste of the individual designers and their selection of my ideas and their own variations. When I open a new shop I spend a great deal of time on promotion and publicity – an important aspect which I find fascinating.

☐ I was asked to design two new shops, one for men and one for women, with a coffee area linking the two, for a Piccadilly store. Our brief was to make it as unlike a shop as possible – rather to create the effect of being in someone's living-room. Paul Hull and I decided to use roman shades at the windows, a geometric carpet on the floor, and books, ashtrays, objects and table lamps. My favourite parabolic spotlights controlled by rheostat switches created dramatic lighting.

☐ The coffee area, where people could relax between 'His' and 'Hers' departments, was placed on a mezzanine balcony with an updated form of Chinese Chippendale balustrade. At the bottom of the staircase leading to the balcony I used two brown tweed-covered wing chairs.

☐ I used dark, masculine colours in the men's department to give it an uncommercial atmosphere. Since it was on both the ground and lower ground floor I felt it needed even more dramatic lighting. It contains a big, comfortable sofa and a low table flanked by wooden obelisks, china balls and lamps.

☐ What I wanted to achieve in the women's shop was the minimum of clutter with a great feeling of openness. It is very unusual for a store to have vast windows facing due south so I felt it important to respect the airiness of the volume. A pair of elbow chairs upholstered in a pale, feminine blue flank a small table covered in a blue-and-white cotton print; they echo the pretentious gilt armchairs of the pre-war salons, but give an updated feeling of the present. The cashier's window facilitates shop surveillance.

□ A leading Brussels couturier wanted to move
to a new location and consulted me from the very
first, so that I was involved in every aspect of the new
building, including its design. I advised that there
should be no colour in the showroom at all, so
nothing would distract customers from the
merchandise itself. The ground floor needed to be
warm and busy, with plenty of goods on view, yet
with a disciplined atmosphere at the same time. I
devised a floor of granite blocks separated by
ebonized wood, slightly smoked glass windows and
versatile ceiling lighting. On the first floor, where dress
shows are held, the scheme was very empty and
neutral, making an ideal background for the display of
a couture collection. Models appear out of a stainless-
steel-clad square archway and parade up and down
the three-sided modelling area; there I used a
geometric carpet, roman shades in white with black
trimming and stainless-steel chairs with black
upholstery.

Carpets and fabrics

□ I first started designing carpets in 1960 because there were no patterned ones available which I liked. The first two were for my own house in the country. Then I began to design them for individual clients. At a later stage they were manufactured in quantity for the American and British markets.
□ I basically work in four carpet qualities. The most luxurious is the pure wool sculpted carpet which I generally use as a rug with plain or patterned borders. Then there is the fine needlepoint texture of Brussels weave which adapts superbly to

small, tight, geometric designs. The third quality is velvet-smooth wool pile which is good for contract use. The fourth is hand-tufted, extremely deep carpeting made in the Philippines; it is particularly suitable for large boardrooms or large rooms in historic houses because it resembles English Aubusson.

☐ The practical advantage of a patterned carpet is that it shows marks and wear far less than a plain carpet; even now, when I am using a plain carpet, I nearly always add a contrasting border.

I am always looking for total simplicity and practicality in modern design.

Today there are far too many good fabrics, carpets and wallpape

and not enough good ones available to everyone.

Expensive antiqued velvet is hideous yet plain coar

I *hate* satin, particularly when it has designs printed on it.

vailable to the few

hen is inexpensive and elegant.

☐ I designed my first fabric in 1963
for my St Leonard's Terrace house.
Goods and Chattels saw it and
commissioned me to do a range for
them. They were floral damasks and
formal geometrics but on unusual
textures. Then in the later 1960s I
designed a very large range of
geometric fabrics and papers for a
New York company and a smaller
range for an English one.

☐ My present collection – though
we often reprint old designs for
clients – is of small colour-
coordinated geometric designs and
some large torn-paper formal and
floral motifs.

LEARN SOME TRICKS FROM Mr HICKS

INDOOR INFORMATION

DH IS decorating Dan's bayfront villa on Star Island and popped in for a progress check after addressing the National Home Fashions League during the High Point (N.C.) furniture market.

If neighbors want to know who dreamed up that bright apricot exterior of Dan Paul's house, DH did. Seems that in the tropics you mix a super-bright color, paint the house once, let Nature do the rest. From then on you just re-white the woodwork.

Having cocktails chez Paul when David Hicks is there is

you do ... goodby" ... doors slam in house and carport. Conversation floats in the air like confetti.

UNFLAPPABLE DH chatted easily until his turn came to grab a suitcase and run. He said he is four things — author (his fifth decorating book is just out); interior decorator; interior designer (hotels, etc., where he grapples with structural problems); and product designer.

David Hicks towels, sheets, carpets, fabrics, tiles and even neckties are available to shoppers. Doesn't Mr. H. fear that

Turn to Page 4D

NEW YORK.—International interior designer David Hicks appears to be out to derail the Orient Express...the detailed pattern-on-pattern motif which notable U.S. converters have boarded for the spring '71 market.

Stopped in the offices of Hystron Fibers, Inc., the super suave originator of the "gutsy geometric look" coldly dismissed the notion that Far Eastern-hippie inspired patterns are destined to be a major design movement next year.

Nor, he insisted, is he perturbed by prognostications of converters and retailers here that geometrics are on a train to oblivion.

"As a pattern gendre, I don't think geometrics have begun to penetrate the U. S. market," he declared, adding that he is similarly unimpressed with hippie influences on design trends.

"If geometrics are dead, I'm amused at the number of copies of my look which I spot around your market."

HICKS, AS NOTED earlier in HOME FURNISHINGS DAILY, is working with Hystron to produce a comprehensive line of decorative home fabrics using Trevira polyester. To be sold in Trevira

boutiques in stores around the country—the line won't be shown here until February "because I think the January market is a bore"—the new Hicks collection bears patterns which are now stamped "top secret."

While he indicated that it is unlikely that his new designs will stray into Oriental configurations, Hicks did imply that they should serve to rev up any wilting interest in geometrics.

"This is an all-embrassing concept," he elaborated. "Thus my new looks will be entirely original. Of course, I never do the same thing twice."

As for colors in his new collections, Hicks asserted that he is of similar catholic taste. "Dark colors, rich colors, pale colors—I'll use them all."

HIPPIES AND the hard drug scene came in for some harsh words from the very English designer, however. For one thing, Hicks took issue with those who claim to see a relationship between drugs, hippies and current fabric design trends.

"I don't like hippies," he asserted. "Their design influence? In way-out boutiques, perhaps...but that's about it."

The Hystron office where the jet-setting Hicks spends about two days a month opened a library of Trevira fabrics this week. It is said to contain the best of a cross section from home furnishings mills, knitters, converters, O-T-C and apparel fabrics.

Hicks Here, There, Everywhere

Continued From 1D :

such proliferation may detract from his prestige as a beautifier of Beautiful People's abodes? Not at all.

When you're an in-law of the British royal family, and recently designed apartments in Windsor Castle for Princess Anne and Prince Charles, you don't need to be a snob. On the contrary, as a product designer he finds it helpful to do an occasional house for people who tremble at the thought of $10-a-yard fabric.

"HOW ELSE should I keep in tune with popular tastes? he asks sensibly.

"Britwell," the 17th-18th Century manor house is home to David and Lady Pamela. "Britwell" is halfway between London and Oxford in the deep countryside, not to be confused with the suburbs. It is pure Hicks, sophisticated but relaxed, embellished with DH products and old treasures. (A door into the library is the end panel of a screen. When it closes behind you — no door!) There's a peacock squawking in the garden, and

a full staff of servants in the house.

"I tell the butler, the chauffeur and the rest that we're all a team and our job is to impress the visiting client," confided DH. (For some reason, well-fixed Europeans think they have to explain having more than one servant to an American.)

THAT something old in Dan Paul's house, by the way, the poignant little mummy case with brown-wrapped inmate snuggled within, is not a DH touch.

Dan brought it with him from his former home on Key Biscayne.

The Mountbatten clan is a close one. The Hickses have two girls and a boy. Lady Pamela's sister, Lady Patricia Brabourne, and husband Lord John Brabourne, the filmmaker, have seven. They all share a vacation house on Eleuthera in the Bahamas and go there every March, plus Grandfather Mountbatten.

The youngsters (great-great-grandchildren of Queen

Victoria) spill onto the beaches. There's no telephone. "It's marvelous," breathes DH.

His life is one transoceanic flight after another ... Greece ... Australia ... New York ... and he has learned to use the time

sketching desig on a current se grams. If yo enough to have overnight chez might design a monogram as a gift. He does that

David Hicks puts design and color to work for the internationally famous. He's currently working as a home furnishings fabric design consultant. Insert illustrates his favorite motif — geometric designs.

British Interior Designor Fast And Expensive

Need an Interior Decorator at $1,000 an Hour?

British interior designer David Hicks is an original who puts design and color to work for the internationally famous. He's currently at work as a home furnishings design consultant for the makers of Trevira polyester on co-ordinated fabric designs for the American mass market. Insert illustrates his favorite motif—geometric designs.

Decorated Prince Charles' apartment

His 'grand' fee is for 'spiffing up'

British decorator with a Midas touch

Need To Consult An Interior Decorator— At $1,000 An Hour

Interior Decorator's Fee A Spur To Do-It-Yourself

Hicks's magic wand

By Marilyn Hoffman

New York

David Hicks, that impeccably tailored English designer-decorator, is having a campaign to take the American home. His invasion, involving his total design approach, will be aptly called the "Hicksonian Environment." And it will be launched in 25 major stores in the United States in October 1971, and thereafter in some other countries.

His target is clearly the homemaker of moderate means who can pay $5.98 per yard for the fabrics of Hystron polyester he is designing for Everfast, and who will appreciate the "prefabricated" decorative assemble and Hicks's guidance in putting it together. The aforesaid "environment" will also include velvets and upholstery jacquards by La France, rugs by Regal, tablecloths and napkins by J. P. Stevens, Nettlecreek bedspreads, modern furniture by Thayer Coggin, and traditional furnishings by Heritage. All touched by the Hicks wand, of course.

The en masse American will be a new field for Mr. Hicks who heretofore has largely turned his talent on the homes, offices, and watering places of the rich and famous, including British royalty and aristocracy. He jets hither and yon at dizzying pace, and currently is working on British Steel Corporation offices in New York, private houses in Florida, Boston, Sydney, Australia, and Paris. Plus a 38-bedroom chateau in Switzerland, a penthouse in Athens, offices in South Africa, a dress shop in Brussels, and a 17th-century home in Masstrich, Holland. His design studio in London, with a staff of 12, has also worked out plans for the new City of London Club.

An international clientele, waiting bated checkbook in hand, seeks the designer's elite services. The Hicksonian look for Hystron is being projected over the next five years, and David Hicks predicts that "in ten years' time we'll still be expanding and refining."

Much emphasis will be put on the geometric patterns he has already made famous in his rugs for Norman and in his wallpaper design. The collection for Everfast will include, he says, geometrics (but certainly), geoforms, and geoflowers, all stylized patterns in the crisp, clean colors he favors, a greige background color that he calls "Coco Chanel," and a combination of soft light brown, orange, and pink. He sees a saturated strawberry pink and a pure aqua blue as strong comeback colors for backgrounds. The rich brown with which he painted his own drawing room walls in London appears and reappears in carpet and fabric designs.

He feels that color must have force and character. "Color means more to me than any other raw material," he says. "Most people are afraid of color, but it is one of the most exciting and rewarding things and can easily create a complete transformation in any room."

When "the look" debuts, Mr. Hicks will tour stores, speak to the customers, and show them via slide lectures and brochures how to mingle their own personal mix. And a pattern-on-pattern mix it will surely be because that is what the well-known Briton believes in most.

"Pattern on pattern," he says, "gives atmosphere and character. A plain surface can be so boring." We didn't particularly agree, and we believe that few women will be up to properly commingling geometrics, florals, herringbones, and plaids in their own living rooms.

Mr. Hicks insists, however, that he can lead the way to daring mixtures, brought off with style and taste. He thinks "young and fresh," but concedes that some of his fabric designs could conceivably be appropriate for the "middle-aged."

$1,000 an hour

Flamboyant Britisher is 'Midas' of interior design

NEW YORK — (NEA) — Money is tight? Not if you are a client who wants a few apartment rooms or a house in Manhattan, Athens, Paris, Nassau or the Bahamas spiffed up by David Hicks.

Hicks is a phenomenon in a sense. He is a magnificently flamboyant Britisher. Understatement is not his medium. And under the close scrutiny all the drive, flair and self-appreciation hang together for this international leader in interior design.

On his corporation conference room bulletin board was scribbled: "Midas Hicks, Esquire."

IN THE shadow of the "Midas" sign, Hicks revealed he was in the city to promote his new assignment as design consultant for Hystron Fibers' home furnishings division.

"As you know, I work fast," he explained. "My fee is $1,000 an hour as an interior design consultant. A woman here wanted me to consult on four rooms for a Fifth Avenue apartment. After we talked

for four hours I reminded her of the fee and she said, 'Keep talking. It's so fascinating. I'll pay extra.'"

To him this pinpointed a basic difference in approach to decorating the home of an American as opposed to that of a European.

"IN EUROPE, most people know what atmosphere they want," Hicks says. "Men and women in the U.S. tell me, 'My God. What am I paying you for? You're the professional. That's why I came to you for advice.'"

Hicks is making financial tracks with this American attitude. He will help direct design and color use of Trevira polyester in upholstery, carpeting, decorative fabrics, wall coverings, bedding, curtains and draperies, area and bath rugs. Some of his fine design thoughts should surface during the January home furnishings market in Chicago and be in the stores for Mrs. Average Consumer in Spring '71.

These will show a strong geometric design trend. He is fond of geometrics because they are classical and helped move them into mass prominence almost 10 years ago in British carpet and rug design.

HICKS LIKES pattern-on-pattern — a room in his Oxfordshire country home is brown, black and yellow Victorian with 18 different patterns. This, the 41-year-old businessman shares with his wife, Lady Pamela Mountbatten, and their two girls and a boy. She is the daughter of Lord Mountbatten of Burma and a cousin of the Queen. Hicks recently redecorated Prince Charles' four-room apartment in Buckingham Palace.

"I want to make geometrics palatable to the general public," he said. "I would like to work with mobile homes. I'd put in geometrics but they would soft and wooing."

He definitely is thinking in terms of pastels, such as faded banana yellow and pale almond green, and shifted the color of his dark, lacquered living room in one of his homes to white. His summer house in the south of France is "all whitewash, with rushes, modern paintings and antiquities, while the master bathroom in our Chelsea (London) townhouse has a clear Plexiglas tub, walls covered in bronze khaki Trevira and a wood-burning fireplace."

HIS PROBLEM in getting his color and design thoughts into more moderately priced homes is reaching the "midbuyer or home furnishings coordinator.

"The man on the street generally has no taste, good or bad, and home furnishings suffers from 'the ditherers' who don't know which way to go," he explained.

"I did tea trays that retailed for $3 about three years ago. I saw them in the pantries of my moneyed and titled friends. Good design is recognized anywhere, no matter the price."

☐ In 1968 I designed a range of towels and sheets for an American company. Their versatility is demonstrated by the variety of ways in which we displayed them. Pattern, if it is intrinsically well conceived, should be suitable for almost any application.

Flair

David Hicks — interior deco for the Royal Family

PERSONALITY
Jane Fraser

DAVID HICKS, interior designer extraordinary, who has decorated the homes of princes and paupers (the palaces of sheiks and semis in the less salubrious areas of London), is back in Johannesburg. "I want to have a look at my South African shop and get away from all the snow. I haven't seen the sun since about August."

He's an attractive man — with that superbly groomed suavity peculiar to British aristocracy; and is erudite in the unhesitant manner of those totally sure of their own ground.

One of Mr Hicks's latest and most interesting — to many anyway — assignments is for Princess Anne. He is to carry through the design of her new home in Gatcombe Park.

Royalty too, is apparently feeling the pinch, for the Royal command is "Low Budget".

Of course he's not giving away any royal secrets and the how's, why's and what's of Her home will remain a secret, for the time being, anyway. Mr Hicks neatly parries such inquisitiveness with, "I admire her tremendously." One assumes he admires too, the taste of this strong-willed young lady with the uncommonly good seat.

There again, Princess Anne is no stranger to David Hicks. They are related by way of his marriage to Lady Pamela Mountbatten, besides which, the Queen had him decorate living quarters for Charles and Anne at Buckingham Palace.

It's largely a jet-setting life. "I visit each of my shops at least once a year and I try to be in a different capital for each birthday. Usually, whichever restaurant I celebrate at does a new room in my honour."

All this and a family man too. "I'm besotted with my children. In fact I've always loved children. When I was about 16 I used to stand outside Woolworths and talk to the babies in their prams. Irate mothers would chase me off, convinced I was up to no good."

There are three Hicks children. "The eldest, Edwina," said David, "is exquisite. Underdeveloped, thank God and marvellous long legs. She's going to be a great lady — speak beautiful French and travel round the world with me, working in my shops."

Lounging in one of "his" chairs, juxtapositioned in front of the crucifix of H's that is his trademark, languidly chain smoking over lunch or expounding gently but firmly on decor, David Hicks exudes confidence, injects life.

● Tomorrow: David Hicks gives some ideas and advice on decorating.

DAVID HICKS

COVADONGA O'SHEA
PIMENTEL

Ha pasado por Madrid como un relámpago. Viene a decorar una casa en Puerta de Hierro. A primera hora de la mañana tiene una reunión en Casa y Jardín, empresa con la que piensa trabajar en el futuro. En el bolsillo, un billete de avión para volver a Londres a mediodía. A pesar de su horario apretado, David Hicks encuentra una hora para compartir sus ideas sobre esa técnica y ese arte, nada fácil, de la decoración de interiores. Y lo hace con calma, como si en un tiempo indefinido no tuviese otra cosa que hacer, sino contestar a todas mis preguntas. Gran resorte psicológico y temperamental de los ingleses, que saben compaginar la máxima tensión interior con la calma más aplastante.

Habla despacio, escucha con interés, sonríe plácidamente, posa sin pestañear cuantas veces se le pida. En tres meses ha dado la vuelta al mundo, no por una apuesta a lo Philleas Fogg, sino para resolver una serie de proyectos de mucha envergadura y no menos millones de libras. Pesan sobre sus hombros trabajos encargados por el Gobierno de Australia y de Londres, por particulares de Miami o de Suiza, por empresas textiles o por los tradicionales propietarios del Club de Hombres de la Ciudad de Londres. Encargos que le preocupan, aunque por su modo de hablar se adivina que disfruta tanto con cada uno, que más parece que se trata de un «hobby» que de una gran responsabilidad. Me asegura, sin embargo, y se lo acepto, que el trabajo es duro. Exige una dedicación completa, física e incluso espiritual, tan total que ni en los mejores momentos de sus vacaciones puede olvidarse de lo que lleva entre manos. Y es natural.

CORADOR INGLES QUE TRABAJA PARA LOS CINCO CONTINENTES

Para un artista, cualquier pequeño aliento de vida, el detalle más insignificante, puede resultar revelador.

—Háblenos del gran secreto de su decoración. Usted es un maestro en todo lo que suponga mezcla audaz de elementos, líneas, diseños y colores. ¿Cómo, cuándo y por qué hizo posible lo que parecía imposible?

—Las primeras ideas sobre decoración las tuve cuando era muy joven. Desde pequeño fui un rebelde, y esa postura vital me influyó de modo decisivo para mi carrera. El gusto de mi padre y de mi madre me aburrían. Y encontraba igual de aburridos los cuartos de los hoteles, las casas de nuestros amigos, todo lo que iba viendo a mi alrededor. Lo encontraba formal, conservador, triste.

—¿Cuántos años tenía cuando empezó a trabajar?

SIGUE

Royal interior for David Hicks

I HEAR that David Hicks is to do the interior decoration of Gatcombe Park, the house in Gloucestershire bought by the Queen for Princess Anne and her husband.

Other customers of his have included Helena Rubenstein, the owners of the Q.E.2, the British Steel Corporation, the film director John Schlesinger and the Soviet airline Aeroflot.

Hicks's latest work has been in Northern Ireland: the renovation of Baronscourt, home of Lord Hamilton, former Ulster Unionist M.P. for Fermanagh and South Tyrone.

Carpets and fabrics

1. The entrance to my London shop in Jermyn Street: four room settings are divided by the H logo which is made of parquet floor laid in a chevron pattern pointing towards the centre of the logo. The background to the parquet is door-matting.

2. A black-and-white geometric stair carpet continues the non-colour theme of a granite and ebonized wood floor in Belgium.

3. One of my small-patterned fabrics is used for the curtains of a dentist's waiting-room; on the octagonal table is a black pottery lamp with a black-lacquered shade. The floors throughout the consulting-rooms are carpeted in my Queen Bee design in black, white and beige.

4. The entrance hall of the same dentist's surgery in Upper Wimpole Street has red walls. On the podium is a piece of sculpture lit by an uplighter.

5. I used a relief carpet in white wool for the floor of a white drawing-room which I created for a client in Miami. On either side of the white jacquard-covered sofa are Louis XV chairs covered in bronze-coloured silk velvet. White Parson's tables hold objects and a palm tree. The room is cool and elegant – ideal for a hot climate.

6. For an advertising agency's reception area I designed a carpet incorporating their logo. I placed two Benson sofas opposite each other, and, at the far end, a dramatic scarlet-lacquered reception desk. The walls are covered in brown tweed.

7. My Y-patterned carpet used for the entrance hall and staircase of a London flat.

1

3

2

4

5

6

7

Product design

□ My first product design was in the early sixties when I started doing geometric carpets. Although they were special orders for clients they were soon being sold in New York and other cities to interior designers and private individuals. I began designing fabrics in 1964 and at about the same time designed some tin trays for Goods and Chattels in London which sold incredibly well. Much more recently I did an inexpensive range of wallpapers for an English company. Although the designs were a success the manufacturers did not reprint them, so I have now produced my own range of wallpapers. I devised a collection of plain furnishing fabrics in sixty-nine colours several years ago which continues to sell steadily.

□ The Bayerische Motoren Werke (BMW) asked me to style the interiors of two cars for a motor show in London. One was a small model, a family or second car, which I did with a puce exterior, aubergine tweed upholstery and a shocking pink and aubergine patterned carpet – it looked very stylish. The second was a large executive-type car which I did in very, very dark, slightly metallic bronze on the outside, with bronze suede on the fascia and dashboard and bronze löden upholstery. The idea was that people would order a special car from BMW and that I would be available as consultant. They could either have a car exactly as they saw it in the showroom or I would advise on different colour schemes. It was a very exciting job and the cars looked terrific but alas the idea proved to be impracticable due to the high cost of custom finishing.

□ My Japanese associates have formed the David Hicks Association of Japanese Manufacturers of which I am president. It is a very efficient, possibly unique organization, the members of which meet once a month in Tokyo to co-ordinate colours for the coming season so that if, for instance, men's ties are being designed in certain colours, shoes, towels and so on can be colour co-ordinated. We do very little basic shape designing, although we have created a whole range of handluggage and shoes. Our contribution is to apply pattern and style. A new company joins the association about every three month on average and among the products that we have already designed are costume jewellery, bedroom slippers, dressing-gowns, head-scarves, belts, cigarette lighters, luggage, umbrellas, golf shirts, cardigans, socks, men's ties, handbags, wallets and cuff-links. I would not approve of a handbag made in Japan with my name on it if the manufacturers had misinterpreted the design or altered it detrimentally. Everything they have done so far I have liked, for it is of good quality. I have a British representative in Japan who keeps a close eye on what they are doing from week to week.

☐ I was probably the first private individual in England to have an all-black car inside and out with black glass in the back and rear door windows. The roof lining and seats were done in black box-cloth and there was a black carpet. I suppose I am responsible for every car with black windows that you see today. All-black interiors in modern production cars are quite popular but they are done in the wrong materials. There is black plastic on the dashboard and a sticky black herring-bone, velvety jacquard-woven cloth on the seats. Often these interiors have a grey roof lining which is quite wrong.

☐ I would love to design a standard production car because I think the level of design in most modern motor cars is pretty abysmal. The detailing inside a Rolls Royce, for example – the steering wheel, the controls, the door handles – is all wrong. On the other hand, the Renault 5 is very good for a small car. The new Rover shows thought although it is not elegant and has too many hard areas inside which are unusable, as does the Range Rover. I now have a Ford Granada station wagon with a black interior and discreet H signs on the doors.

☐ There are still many areas in which I want to work. I would like to design jacquard weaves and I am about to do a collection for a Belgian manufacturer. I would like to design china and silver – all modern silver is too heavy. I would like to design real jewellery – I have done some for my wife – and interiors for trains, buses and coaches.

☐ I have always gone into product design to fill gaps. I went into carpet design because there were no patterned carpets on the market that were acceptable to me. I did the wallpaper collection because the manufacturers wanted something special in addition to their run-of-the-mill commercial collection.

Product design

1

4

1. Bedroom slippers on which I applied
geometrics and my signature and logo – one of our
best-selling lines in Japan.
2/3. Handbags and wallets produced in Japan to my
designs.
4. Prototypes of cigarette lighters that I designed in
various metallic and lacquer finishes.
5. There is a large demand in Tokyo and other cities in
Japan for kitchen aprons and we have designed over
fifty of these.
6. I designed an alphabetic, geometric range of ties for
the American and English markets and have recently
redesigned them for Japan. They sell extremely well.
7. Silk scarves and cotton handkerchiefs based on my
logo and geometrics.
8. A collection of belts which I designed.
9. The interior of the BMW using brown suede and a
brown and black geometric carpet as a soothing foil to
the dark bronze/brown exterior.

7

3

6

9

Product design

□ A few years ago I designed for a large company a whole kitchenware range decorated with our geometrics and including, for example, tin wastepaper baskets. Although they were very inexpensive, they did not capture the market.

Drawing-rooms

☐ I find that many people are confused about what to call the room in which they sit or entertain. The word lounge is appropriate only for an area in an airport or an hotel. Drawing-room suggests that the house has another reception room other than a dining-room, and the name dates from the eighteenth century when ladies withdrew from the gentlemen after dinner.
In an apartment the best term to use is living-room. There are other names such as morning-room, saloon or boudoir, but the are usually only found in large historic houses.
☐ I love proper country-house drawing-rooms with a good chimneypiece, fine cornice and t right proportions, but I also like a living-room in an apartment whi has had the same careful attentic to detail, fireplace mouldings and

☐ In the drawing-room of a nineteenth-century castle in Ireland I endeavoured to re-create some of the atmosphere of the 1870s. William Morris had painted the blue-and-white tiles for the chimneypiece, so I had one of his superb wallpapers reprinted in a series of apricots and beiges. The two Victorian armchairs were re-upholstered, one in chestnut brown tweed, the other in one of my red, white and brown geometric cottons, while I used fig red tweed on the chesterfield sofa. I rehung the seventeenth-century family portraits on the chimneypiece wall; behind the sofa I placed a Paul Nash watercolour under an oil painting by Jack Yeats.

☐ To create a green sitting-room in London I covered the walls in green suede cloth, used green-a white and plain green coverings the furniture and a textured gree carpet on the floor. I used one lo roman shade at the window and designed a simple white marble fire-surround with a smoked gla interior.

furniture arrangements.
Atmosphere, colour, hanging of
pictures, furniture, flowers,
objects and lighting are the
ingredients one needs to make a
stylish drawing-room full of
character. I know many people
who, with or without a decorator,
have produced good drawing-
rooms, while I know many more
who, usually without an interior
designer, have failed to do so.

□ A number of the rooms shown in
this book have television sets in
them – some portable, others large
sets concealed under side tables.
The great problem when including
a television set in a living-room is to
make sure that people can see the
screen easily. I always try to arrange
the chairs as attractively as
possible, bearing in mind this
limitation to aesthetic planning.

□ In the gallery of an Irish
house I arranged three seating
areas. I used white paint on the
elaborate plasterwork ceiling by
William Vitruvius Morrison, and
picked out the walls in beige and
white. Accent colours of brilliant
buttercup yellow, pale sugar pink,
cerulean blue and chamois give
excitement in a beige scheme.

should have been this deep

should have been narrower

日 発行　昭和45年6月15日第三種郵便物認可

第 68 号

プレス

回20日発行一

. . . Footnote on the high cost of making movies: David Hicks, London's No. 1 interior designer (and son-in-law of Lord Mountbatten, an identification he must be sick of), flew in from London last wkend just to upgussy Russ Keil's house in Tiburon for a few scenes in "Petulia." What makes this funny is that Director Richard Lester says he decided to shoot "Petulia" here to get out of his new house near London, which David is also decorating. I guess that makes it funny . . .

☐ A large living-room in New
South Wales with a dining corner
has walls of painted brick, a slate
floor and a fireplace made of natural
wood. For the windows I used
roman shades in pale cerulean blue
with a dark brown inset border.

☐ I painted the walls of this Syd
drawing-room a pale French gre
and used beige and white cottor
for covering the fine eighteenth-
century elbow chairs. In the
summer the sofas have pink and
white geometric cushions and ir
winter cushions in rich, glowing
colours.

□ It is sometimes interesting to use the raw materials of a house, if one can get down to them. In this drawing-room the plasterwork had to be stripped off the walls and, since the brickwork was extremely pleasing, I left it natural. Against the raw brick I placed a beautiful pine and marble eighteenth-century fireplace, and I used Siamese silks in various reds and pinks for the curtains and sofas.

Fireplaces

□ Any room that has a fireplace should be planned around it, for it provides a splendid focal point. I have worked on rooms that once had a chimneypiece where I have reinstated an old one and modern apartments where I have designed a chimneypiece specifically for the room. The chimney-shelf of a fireplace is a marvellous place on which to make an effective arrangement of a clock, objects and flowers. The basket for the logs or coal container provides yet another design decision and many people enjoy the cosy comfort of a club fender – personally I do not.

□ I like to have a real fire burning in the fireplace – always a most welcoming sight. One of my great delights is to put a small twig of juniper into the fire for two minutes and then, having blown out the flame, carry it round the room because the smoke smells absolutely delicious. In the country by far the best firewood is well-dried beech logs; oak and ash are also good. In Ireland we burn the turf which, although causing a good deal of dust, does have the most wonderful smell. Never burn pine. In the early autumn I always put my prunings – especially my taller herbs – on the fire because then the first fire of late autumn is wonderfully aromatic. This gives me so much pleasure that I now bundle up bunches of tarragon and even choisya in readiness for the next fire. Lavender too can be delicious on a fire and the stalks are as good as the

1

seed heads that you probably put into pot-pourri or a container on their own.

☐ For those who live in cities there are some acceptable gas log fires on the market now. In my London rooms I have one fireplace in which I burn smokeless fuel and another, in the bedroom, which I do not use. I have filled the opening with a panel covered in pleated cotton – an old idea often used on the Continent in summer.

1. A nineteenth-century Louis XV-style fireplace holds a Roman bust and some eighteenth-century blue and white porcelain. Two Louis XVI *fauteuils* at the puzzle table are covered in tapestry, while the eighteenth-century English chairs on either side of the chimney have been freshly gilded and covered in pale salmon pink ultra suede. I de-electrified the candle sconces, and for parties real candles are lit. The floor is covered in wall-to-wall jute matting. The section of glass under the top of the fireplace prevents the fire smoking.

2. A high eighteenth-century wooden chimneypiece is adorned with three family crests in carved and gilded wood. I placed the busts, which I found in a cellar of the house, round the walls of this entrance hall. The chairs are early seventeenth-century Italian, covered in their original damask. The walls were painted in dragged apricot of two tones, with the mouldings picked out in white.

2

☐ An Edwardian fireplace, possibly designed by Sir Edwin Lutyens, against geranium pink felt walls. On the mantelpiece are a variety of interesting objects which enliven each other through their unexpectedness as neighbours: a modern Indian terracotta tiger, a bizarre nineteenth-century pottery clock, a dried iris pressed between two sheets of glass, a small panel by Rex Whistler and a sculpture from Tahiti. The nineteenth-century fire-irons are both practical and decorative.

☐ The honey-coloured silk-covered walls, above the white-painted dado and chair rail, make a splendid foil for the black-and-white, early eighteenth-century English marble chimneypiece in this Sydney house. Above it hangs an early Australian landscape.

☐ I designed this white marble fireplace for a small London flat. I could not widen the interior because of the flues from the flats below, so I used mirror to give the chimneypiece classical proportions. Two empire swan chairs face two others invisible behind the camera. Dried flowers and miscellaneous objects make up the various chimney- and tablescapes.

☐ My Spanish associate, Paco Muñioz, devised a stainless-steel chimney breast as a foil for an early nineteenth-century fire grate. He hung a mid-nineteenth-century Bavarian glass-framed mirror on it which makes a splendid contrast with the Colombo chair. My geometric carpet with a plain border completes the scheme.

1. An exotic partly gilded carved pine fireplace designed by Batty Langley in 1742 holds two porphyry tole urns, surmounted by an early nineteenth-century gothic bracket on which stands a carved wooden peacock.

2. In an unimportant guest bedroom in a Victorian house with few objects I had to make the most of what was available – a Victorian jug and a pair of candlesticks. I hung a reproduction gilt mirror above the fireplace and flanked it with two eighteenth-century black-and-white engravings.

3. Above a scrubbed stone fireplace with tiles decorated by William Morris I made a symmetrical arrangement of pictures, prints and Victorian pottery.

4. A Victorian pitch-pine fireplace has glazed tiles again hand-painted by Morris. On either side of a copy of the Lely painting of Sir William Temple hang portraits of him and his wife in old age. On the fireplace is a pair of eighteenth-century pewter plates, an Edwardian oak clock, bleached oak columns and two copies of the Chevaux de Marly. The wallpaper is also by William Morris.

1

2

3

4

5. In a rather dreary room with a plain Victorian stone fireplace I created a little style by using one of my geometric wallpapers.

☐ A selection of formalized floral
designs, many of which are still
being manufactured; some of them
never got beyond the prototype
stage but I will find a use for them
one day. I am inspired a great deal
by the past in evolving pattern in
my product design and my most
important source is Owen Jones's
Grammar of Ornament which
records accurately and beautifully
patterns of almost every civilization.

☐ Patterns can give great
atmosphere, as can be seen in the
paintings of Vuillard and Matisse
and earlier in Pre-Raphaelite
interiors. I love pattern and use it a
great deal, especially in carpets.
☐ People are often confused about
how to mix pattern with pattern. It
is difficult to lay down hard and
fast rules but, generally speaking,

different patterns can be used in the
same area, providing they are of
different scale and are colour
co-ordinated, in other words at
least one colour must appear in
both fabrics. What I look for is
affinity and this can be found in
stock fabrics, wallpapers and
carpets. Colour and design are the
important connections to make.

Pattern

□ I tend to use modern fabrics of my own design because I now create so many, but inevitably I often resort to others, particularly for antique or traditional designs.
□ The fabric in the illustration below left is a black and ochre late Victorian glazed print which I had reprinted for my own use. The silk patchwork cushion in red, yellow and blue was made from a Ghanaian traditional garment. Another cushion is covered in a reprint of early nineteenth-century *toile de Tarascon*. The pale ochre, black and khaki vegetable-relief velvet cushion was formerly in the collection of Mrs Cole Porter and was given to me by Billy Baldwin. The two Turkish embroidery cushions look attractive together because they have similar colours but different designs.

These ashtrays, tobacco and cigarette jars are basically three-dimensional patterns. They were designed for a cigarette-lighter company in Japan where every top executive has a smoking set on his table. So far this range has not been put into production.

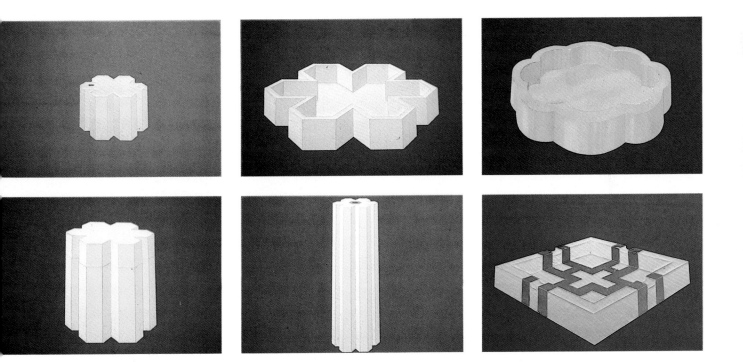

Flowers and plants

□ I love arranging flowers. When I am walking through a wood or down a country lane I pick wild flowers at random and make an arrangement in my hand just for the sheer pleasure of seeing different colours, textures and leaves together. I have always massed flowers together – perhaps a great bunch of Peace roses, perhaps a huge bowl of tulips all of one colour or an enormous spring bouquet, tightly packed. I have certain set methods which are easily copied and I am delighted and flattered when they are. But it should be remembered that it is far more interesting to develop your

own personal style in flower arranging.

☐ Flowers and leaves are to me an essential part of an interior. Even the smallest city garden can provide leaves to cut: variegated laurel, for instance, is an extremely handsome shrub from which to make an architectural mass of green in winter when flowers are not available; choisya is another incredibly useful shrub all through the year. Simplicity in the container and the arrangement is very important. I do not particularly like elaborate baroque flower arrangements which are the delight of professional florists.

☐ The relationships of a flower arrangement to other objects on the same table and pictures on the wall above is very important. Sometimes I use a small posy under a large painting and sometimes a large bouquet over small objects. It is the element of surprise that creates pleasure in this change of scale and mood. I almost never try to repeat an arrangement and vary my containers a great deal.

Flowers and plants

1. It is often an attractive idea to put flowers on the floor for this, after all, is how you see them in the garden. Here a large bunch of pink and yellow chrysanthemums in a metal container has been placed inside a rush-matting basket.
2. *Iris stylosa*, although short-lived, have great magic since their flowering period is from the end of November until mid-March. These have been placed under a brown pottery lamp on a snakeskin patchwork table beside an Etruscan red tweed-covered sofa.
3. A mass of dried gypsophila fills a late seventeenth-century blue-and-white Nevers vase, while beside it a

1

2

5

6

resh bunch of choisya has been stuffed into a modern Swedish amber glass cylinder. The Regency table also holds a nineteenth-century wooden model of Giotto's campanile in Florence and some small pieces of pottery made by my children.

4. Brilliant blue cineraria placed in front of a scarlet sofa; in the background is a wallpaper of my design in cineraria blue, green and red, based on nineteenth-century Turkish carpets in the Paris shop.

5. A basket containing a sheaf of wheat from our farm stands on a table covered in a cloth made from a traditional Ghanaian robe in silk patchwork given to

me by President Nkrumah; also on the table are two laburnum-wood lamps made in 1910, a bottle made from the same wood and an African basket.

6. Another basket of wheat, this time reflecting the images from the drawings above it by Denis Wirth-Miller.

7. A huge arrangement of dried leaves and flower heads of all sorts stands in a large stone urn on a stone column in my London shop.

8. A large basket of dried seed heads boldly placed on one of my geometric carpets in a Piccadilly store that I partly redesigned.

4

8

235

☐ I have always loathed plastic flowers and would
categorically rule them out. On the other hand, I have
sometimes quite liked flowers made out of gauze or
chiffon. In our shop in Paris we sell ravishing tulips
and carnations made out of very delicate David Hicks
prints; they are of a geometric design in pale yellow
and pale pink, moulded into stiff, life-size shapes.
They are beautifully made and used individually in a
specimen vase they look very effective.
☐ Dried flowers and seed heads are very acceptable –
I particularly like dried giant hemlocks, alliums and
hydrangeas, but it is important to put them away in the
spring and summer months when there are fresh
blooms available from the garden.
☐ I like plants indoors, but there are some such as the
rubber plant that have been seen too often and in a
tired state. A number of interesting plants will grow
happily indoors: for instance, I have a banana plant in
my London bedroom. I also grow sweet-scented
geraniums and other potted plants.

1. Dried mulleins in a large glass cylinder are
effectively silhouetted against a window covered by a
wooden grille.
2. Dried alliums against the light take on a sculptured
quality.
3. Dried hydrangeas in a faded pink used in
conjunction with a separate vase of fresh geraniums.
4. A five-foot-high arrangement of dried hemlock
assumes an almost forest-like quality against the
window.
5. On the corner of a chimneypiece I spotlit an amber
glass vase containing dried alliums.
6. Dried hydrangeas in a square pottery vase have
been placed on two Japanese funerary stands.

1

4

3

6

□ I always enjoy the high standard of flower arranging when I work in the United States. In this Miami house which I redecorated, the flowers were arranged by the local florist to contrast with the walls which I had covered in a striped fabric.

□ An Edwardian panelled room, previously a cold, dull place, has been given personality and warmth by the massed arrangements of leaves and plants and by the red sofas.

1. Artichokes, lime, wild daisies, allium and an orchid leaf compose this arrangement of dried plants placed on a telephone table.
2. I do not spurn artificial flowers entirely. Here I have placed a milliner's shocking-pink silk rose in a polished steel container. Beside the vase is a pressed iris framed between two sheets of clear glass.
3. This banana plant in my London chambers has character, colour and texture. It minds the English winters almost as much as I do but flourishes in the sunny south-west-facing window.
4. *Daphne laureola*, packed tightly into a rectangular white pottery container, gives marvellous textural interest in midwinter.
5. Three white paper flowers made by my children, arranged in a Victorian red and white glass vase.
6. In a textured white cylinder vase an artichoke is in the process of being dried simply by allowing the water to evaporate.

1

4

3

6

□ In a Paris office we used colour in an exciting way: the patterned and plain-bordered carpets relate to the bold colour treatment of the walls. The dazzling object at the end of the corridor is a fire extinguisher framed to look like a precious antiquity.

□ This living-room, which I designed with my Paris associate Christian Badin, has a strong sense of style in the way in which the colour theme – yellow and pink – has been carried right through, with no other colours apart from natural finishes being used.

□ This rather awkwardly designed house in Geneva demanded stylish internal architecture. To make a break between the spacious entrance hall and the large living-room dominated by a fine Buddha I devised floor-to-ceiling vitrines which house a collection of porcelain and antiquities.

□ Real candles used in conjunction with uplighters give this room a very strong sense of style and atmosphere in a Paris apartment.

Bathrooms

□ I am particularly interested in bathroom design and have always taken enormous trouble with all bathrooms, small though they might be. This great interest came about because I had such an uncomfortable period at school, as a student and in the army, as well as being appalled by hotel bathrooms, so that I longed to create really attractive ones. For me they are a very important part of a flat or house. An enormous number of ideas come to me whilst I am lying in the bath in the morning or the evening, so I always have something readily at hand with which to write.

□ Bathrooms, however small, benefit greatly from atmosphere

and this can be achieved by using pattern, pictures, good lighting and planning, interesting colour and wallpaper. Too often the position of the basin, lavatory and bath is dictated by the plumber and little attention is given to finding the right arrangement.

❏ Bathrooms are often too clinical – expensive marble and double basins are to me an anathema, rather like gladioli on the stern of a luxury yacht. The most glamorous bathrooms that I have ever seen, one very traditional and the other very modern, were those of Emilio Terry in Paris and Cole Porter in New York; the latter, designed by William Baldwin, was all grey, scarlet, black and white.

❏ Every time I design a bathroom I try to use a new approach. In this bathroom in Australia I used a local granite for the bath surround, the free-standing rectangular column holding the bath taps and for the vanitory unit. The matt finish of the granite makes an interesting contrast with the satin-finished stainless-steel taps.

Bathrooms

1. A small all-white bathroom in a country house. The simple table and chair are painted white, as is the eighteenth-century mirror, the Meissen candle sconces and even the wicker wastepaper basket. I put the bath in an alcove created by two cupboards, one for the hot water cylinder and the other for linen and towels, and hung white cotton curtains on either side of the bat give character to an otherwise rather plain room. The towel rail at right-angles to the bath, a convenient place for it to be. It i always a luxurious idea to have chair beside the bath.

2. If the room is not too small I li

1

2

4. In a fairly large bathroom in a house in Darling Point, Sydney, I used mirror, both clear and smoked, granite for the bath surround, white-painted screens and a white towelling day bed.

5. For a small country bathroom in New South Wales I devised a roller blind in one of my French small-repeat cottons, and I used blue accessories to continue the colour theme.

4

5

put the bath in the centre. The basin and bath are standard units, the former being set in a pale oak vanitory top, the latter in a similar ush-panelled surround. I ecided to use refurbished old rass taps. I think old taps are, on he whole, more functional and ood-looking, although I do not have any particular prejudice against modern ones; but a really attractive modern bathroom tap has yet to be designed.

3. In a small London bathroom I built in a dressing table and used two Indian lacquered candlesticks to provide really strong light. The walls and ceiling are painted beige.

3

7

6. In my Chelsea bathroom I stretched a vanitory unit between two walls of an alcove and built the top in white laminate. The white oval basin is sunk into it. Hairbrushes and other objects are carefully arranged.

7. In the cloakroom of a London house I separated the serpentine vanitory unit from the lavatory by a smoked-mirror screen. I used brown wrapping paper for the walls with a border of scarlet and aubergine.

Bathrooms

1/2. In a pitch-pine panelled lavatory I retained the early blue-and-white lavatory bowl and original polished mahogany seat. The cistern and exposed plumbing were polished and lacquered.
3. A very modern treatment of a vanitory unit has a large section of mirror lit by theatre make-up bulbs coming directly out of the mirror. A holland blind in a green and white geometric design covers the

1

2

248

window in this all-white bathroom.
4. Early plumbing fittings should be
retained wherever possible. Here
the bath is contemporary with the
late nineteenth-century house and
gives great atmosphere, although
the taps are more recent.

3

4

□ In a tiny London bathroom I painted the walls, ceiling and bookcase the same pale beige, and I placed a telephone near the lavatory for convenience. Books and objects fill the suspended bookcase.

□ For this bathroom in a London hotel suite I used dark aubergine walls, white curtains and a roman shade trimmed in red, and a screen to hide the lavatory. The vanitory unit has a granite top. The Brussels-weave carpet is in aubergine, red, green and white and flows through into the bedroom next door.

□ A rather small cloakroom
at Britwell looked much bigger
after I had hung sporting
mementos, period photographs,
engravings and other memorabilia
on the walls. A *chaise percée*
covers the lavatory. The window
takes up the entire wall over the
vanitory unit, making it necessary
to hinge the mirror.

I dislike brightly coloured front doors – they are
more stylish painted white, black or other dark
colours. I hate wrought iron. I loathe colour used
on modern buildings – it should be inside. I do not
like conventional standard lamps – I prefer
functional floor-standing reading lights

Function is just as important as aesthetics; but there is no reason why, if a problem is properly considered, function should in any way interrupt aesthetics. Very often the practical aspect of an idea can improve the aesthetic pleasure one gets from it. Function dictates design.

1. A painting by Rib Bloomfield is
suspended from a fine square-
section aluminium rail fixed
between the floated ceiling and the
top of the wall. This method of
hanging pictures means that not
only can you easily change them,
but you can also alter their height.
The painting here is hung rather
low because I like to relate
sculpture and pictures to furniture
and groupings of objects. If it were
twelve inches higher it would give a
cold impression – it would be
divorced from the commode and
the objects. I like objects cutting
over the surface: they seem to me
to work together in harmony.
Even the lamp contributes to the
group, for its shiny black-lacquered
card shade and glazed terracotta-
coloured base relate to the colours
in the painting and on the walls.
□ The carpet is one of my new
textured designs. Although the two
reds used in it are different from the
red of the walls, according to my
well-known theory all reds go
together. The tablecloth fabric is
the same as that used on the chairs,
even the legs of which have been
covered.
□ The walls are made of
blockboard panels covered in
Venetian red tweed. In order to re-
cover the walls, or perhaps one
damaged panel, you merely pull the
panel off the wall, rip off the
material and put on some more;
you can even fasten the material
with a staple gun. I have used this
technique in a number of offices
because it is so practical: the walls
can be re-covered overnight.
□ The traditional way of covering
walls in fabric is to batten all the
outer edges of each wall and
then to stretch bump interlining

1

2

over the walls and tack it to the wooden battens. The interlining is then covered in the same way with velvet, cotton, or whatever material is being used. I still prefer to use this method when possible because it gives a marvellous acoustic softness and a tremendous sense of quality and warmth. It is, however, more costly in both labour and materials.

2. For a luxury hotel suite overlooking Hyde Park I commissioned the hard-edged painting hanging above the red and white marble fireplace to go with the colour scheme which I had based entirely on pinks and reds.

3. A picture by Hen Jensen hangs over the side table in a Dutch house that I decorated. As well as the basket of dried flowers, I placed on the table some nineteenth-century china cows which relate very interestingly to the Friesians in the painting.

4. In the living-room of my old London flat I hung some eighteenth-century architectural drawings in a severe geometric arrangement over an Etruscan red tweed sofa. This is a room which worked successfully because of the way that the pictures were hung and lit, because of the patterned carpet and the doors going right up to the ceiling. Two extremely fine Regency chairs with rams' heads have great quality and style, but the room would be equally successful with a pair of traditional chairs of the same shape without the valuable carved heads. The drawings are originals by Sir William Chambers but they could just as well be reproductions from a museum as long as they were framed and hung properly.

□ I like to mix modern paintings with antique furniture as these photographs of my living-room at Britwell show.

□ In the illustration, opposite, a large, hard-edged, scroll-top picture by Bruce Tippett hangs over a mid-eighteenth-century finely carved chimney which holds a Louis XVI French clock, two Neapolitan vases, two Chinese cockerels and a number of small objects. I like the way the clock encroaches over the base of the painting, and the gilded metal is an exciting contrast to the bright colours of the acrylic-painted canvas.

1. On a white-painted George II table with a scagliola porphyry top I placed a seventeenth-century porphyry cylinder with a Swedish porphyry urn on it. The urn overlapping the all-red picture by Festa is to me exciting and I like the casual look of the tooled red-leather scroll cases standing in a cluster near a drawing by De Laszlo of my mother-in-law.

2. The walls of the room are covered in linen woven in a cream and white geometric design. Over a Louis XVI pink chintz-covered sofa hangs a picture of a rainbow by Rib Bloomfield. In front of the sofa, a glass and brass occasional table holds games, books, a bronze Chinese duck and some small animals cast by my children.

1

2

Pictures

☐ I thought up some interesting and varied ways of hanging a particular client's collection of engravings.
☐ In a bedroom I hung eight pictures in an unusual arrangement of six together and two apart.

☐ On an awkward staircase I hung a number of engravings in a step-like way, purposely accentuating the steepness of the stairs; others were grouped together on a landing between some carved wooden garlands.

☐ At the top of the staircase I screwed an engraving to a jib door to diminish its effect. To conceal it still further I hung another picture so that it just covered the head of the door – a traditional trick of interior decoration but still a valid idea in interior design in a modern setting.

Savannah Sound.
David Hicks 1976.

□ There were a number of people in my early life who, through their appreciation of what I was trying to do and their guidance, exercised a great influence on me. The first was a lady watercolourist who taught me at my preparatory school; she taught me to love floating watercolour on to cartridge paper. Then at Farnham Art School Mr Ricards taught me perspective, and a rather strange, formal, graphic way of looking at shapes, and how to use solid poster colour. At Charterhouse Mr Eccart gave me much encouragement and great freedom. I remember creating a model theatre set of an American house in the Deep South and drawing with great pleasure the luscious leaves of a magnolia tree. On reaching the Central School of Art and Design I came under the influence of William Roberts, Keith Vaughan, Meninsky, Jeannetta Cochrane, Sheila Jackson and Herbert Spencer, all of whom had totally different approaches to their own form of painting, illustration, costume design and typography.

□ When I left art school I was convinced that I was not good enough at painting, theatre design, book illustration, costume design or typography to make a career out of any of them. I also felt that those careers would not be sufficiently rewarding financially.

□ But I had at least learned to draw and I had learned to use my eyes. I had learned to select which painters', architects' and draughtsmen's work I admired most. When I finally emerged as an interior designer a couple of years later all that I had distilled from these various influences and all that had fascinated me was extremely useful. I do not believe that any interior designer or product designer can work solely at the drawing board. I think they have got to be able to draw from life, to understand shapes, textures and techniques. Thus when I finally got involved in interior decoration I had very varied resources to draw upon.

□ Apart from sketching briefs for designers and craftsmen I still have phases when I paint and draw – mostly the latter. I did some landscape drawings recently in black and white which I think are quite stylish. Occasionally I paint in gouache but I am often dissatisfied with what I do. Although I am terribly critical of other people I am even more critical of myself.

□ Christmas cards of our house at Great Henny, near Sudbury, which I did when I was fifteen.

□ The drawing opposite is a view of our local village, Savannah Sound, on the island of Eleuthera – one of the few places where I can find time to draw for pleasure. I love the early nineteenth-century houses which still remain there.

261

☐ A black-and-white drawing from Classiebawn Castle looking north across the park towards Mullaghmore, 1977.

☐ A gouache of Sligo Bay looking towards the town of Sligo, 1977.

□ A drawing for my 1958 Christmas card of the Temple at Stoke by Nayland in Suffolk. I rented the Temple, an eighteenth-century fishing lodge at the head of a large formal canal, for a few years before I married.

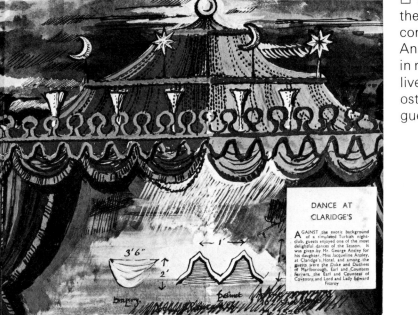

□ My sketch for the central tent in the ballroom at Claridges for the coming-out party for Jacqueline Ansley in 1957. The tent was done in red and blue and at each corner live Nubians stood holding great ostrich fans with which to cool the guests.

DANCE AT CLARIDGE'S

AGAINST the exotic background of a simulated Turkish nightclub, guests enjoyed one of the most delightful dances of the Season. It was given by Mr. George Ansley for his daughter, Miss Jacqueline Ansley, at Claridge's Hotel, and among the guests were the Duke and Duchess of Marlborough, Earl and Countess Ferrers, the Earl and Countess of Coventry, and Lord and Lady Edward Fitzroy

Symbols

□ I use my sign on everything: ties, front doors, writing paper. I used to fly it as a flag on my speedboat in the south of France and still do on my Land Rover in the country. All my Japanese product designs bear the H logo or symbol and I now wear belts, suits, ties and carry attachée cases bearing it. Part of the business of being a stylish designer is projecting your personality and your image on your merchandise and on the public. The sign, monogram or logo is a recognizable and important identification.

□ My sign was designed for me by a local farm manager's son, Richard

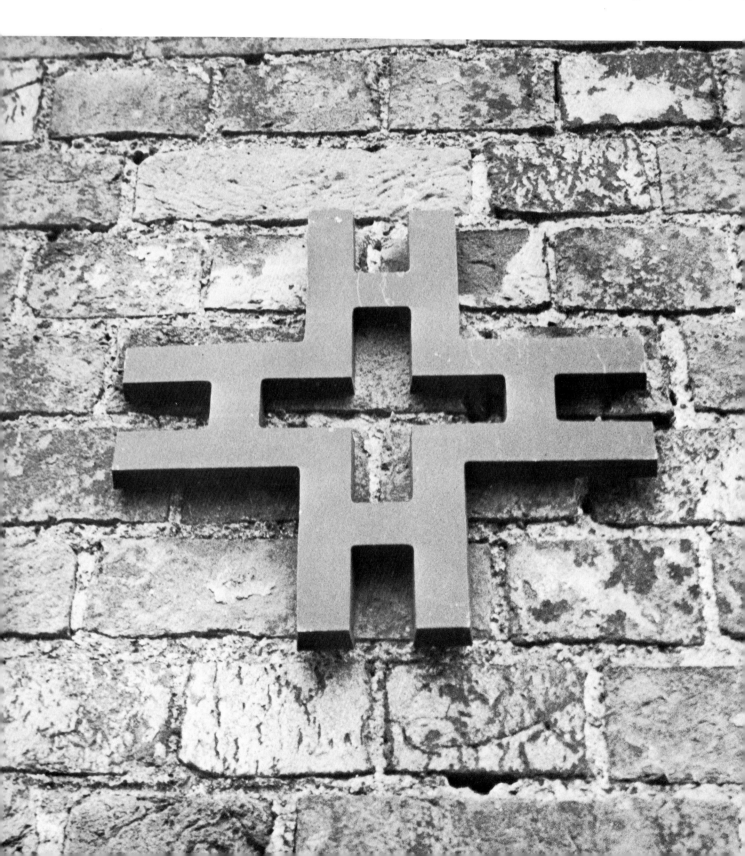

ullen. I got him a job at the age of sixteen and a half with Terence Conran, making tea. He eventually became a successful designer but when he first got the job, he asked me if there was anything he could do to repay me. I suggested that he might try to design a monogram, logo or sign for me, he came up with some alternatives and I chose the present H logo. Monograms and logos are all part of geometrics in which I have an enormous delight: H is a particularly geometric character and lends itself well to pattern.

□ A flat where I lived in Paulton's Square in London had H logos in chromium on the two identical front doors. After I had sold the flat I asked the builder to remove the logos and replace them with suitable numerical plaques. The new owners were determined to keep the logos; they were even prepared to pay for copies to be made because they wanted what they considered to be my signature. The owner of the Octagon House in Britwell similarly wanted an H logo on her home as a signature, which I found very flattering.

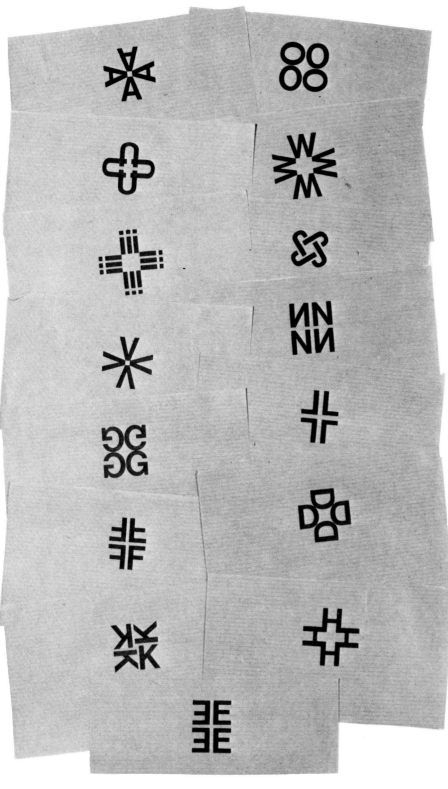

□ Note-blocks with alphabetical geometric headings developed from my tie designs sell well. They all stem from the original logo concept.

Symbols

☐ Because the Japanese had on occasion produced the H logo in the wrong proportions, they issued a design manual which showed how it should be used and, on the end page, how it should not be used.

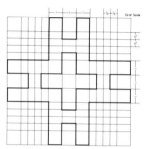

STANDARDIZATION OF DAVID HICKS DESIGNS

This design manual is produced for the visual standardization of the David Hicks symbols and logos basic usage. This manual includes the restrictions for strict standardization of the symbols and the logo for applying to all information required for sales promotion and advertisement including catalogs and all printed materials including bills, as well as all David Hicks merchandise, anything that can be related to the corporate identity.

Thus we hope to increase the David Hicks name penetration to the general public through such standardized designs of symbol and logos by means of the visual approach and at the same time standardize the David Hicks image through all David Hicks merchandise.

〈デービット・ヒックス〉
デザインの統一について。

このデザイン・マニュアルは、デービット・ヒックスのシンボルマーク、ロゴタイプの基本的な使用法について、その視覚的な統一をはかるために制定されたものである。

このマニュアルには、デービット・ヒックスの製品（商品）はもちろん、販売促進、広告宣伝、カタログから伝票類を含むすべての印刷物など、およそコーポレート・アイデンティティにつながるものすべてに、使用時の正確性と統一性を期すための規制が盛りこまれている。

このように統一－（同一化）されたデザインの視覚伝達をとおして、一般大衆にデービット・ヒックスの知名浸透とイメージ創造を期待する一方で、デービット・ヒックスの各種製品間のイメージ同化の相乗効果をねらうものである。

●シンボルマーク

シンボルマークは、ブランドの顔であり象徴であるだけに、視覚的要素の中ではもっとも重要な意味をもっている。

デービット・ヒックスのシンボルマークは、デービット・ヒックス氏自身が創作したものでイニシャルのH文字を幾何学的模様に組合わせて、デザインされている。

このマークは、商標として登録されているが使用に際しては、Ⓡはつけなくともよい。

Corporate Symbol

●Corporate Symbol

The symbol is most important for the visual approach of sales promotion as it is the face of the brand, so to speak.

David Hicks symbol has been designed by David Hicks himself, combining his initial 'H' in geometric form. This symbol has been registered as a trade mark but Ⓡ is not required.

positive   negative

Grid Scale

タイプフェース
ロゴタイプは販売促進に使用する場合

Type specifications

ABCDEFGHIJKLMNOPQRSTUVWXYZ   abcdefghijklmnopqrstuvwxyz   1234567890

ABCDEFGHIJKLMNOPQRSTUVWXYZ   abcdefghijklmnopqrstuvwxyz   1234567890

ABCDEFGHIJKLMNOPQRSTUVWabcdefghijklmnopqrstuvw1234567890

ABCDEFGHIJKLMNOPQRSTUVWXYZ &¥?$ 1234567890

シンボルマーク・ロゴタイプ（サイン・タイプフェース）組み合わせの基本型（仮名文字のデービット・ヒックスを必ず組合わせる）

ロゴタイプ2組み合わせ基本型

David Hicks

●ロゴタイプ1（サインマーク）

このマークもまた、ヒックス氏自身の
筆によるもので、シンボルマークと
共にテーヒット・ヒックスのイメージ
戦略に不可分のものであり、つまり
原則的にはシンボルマークとサイン
マークは一体として用いるものと
する。その基本型については、あとで
述べる

Logo, signature 1

The signed logo is also designed
by David Hicks himself and just
as important as the symbol, for
sales promotion methods by which
we try to promote the David Hicks
image. Therefore the symbol and
the logo shall be used together
as a unit. As for the basic patterns
of usage we shall mention them later.

negative

DAVID HICKS
DAVID HICKS

●ロゴタイプ2

ロゴタイプ2は、サインマークと同時
使用することはない。つまりサイン
マークの代用として、その使用目的や
状況によってロゴタイプ2の方が効果
的な場合にのみ用いる。従って、サイ
ンマークがつねにシンボルマークと
一体化して用いられると同様に、ロゴ
タイプ2もまたかならずシンボルマー
クと共に用いるものとする

Logo, printed 2

This logo shall not be used with
the signature logo.
This shall be used on occasions
and for purposes where we
determine that the printed logo is
more effective than the signature
logo. Therefore as in the case of
the signature, the printed logo
shall always be used with the symbol.

DAVID HICKS

negative

使用例
シンボルマーク・サインマークの組み合わせの基本例

The examples of usage

使用してはいけない例

The examples of non-usage

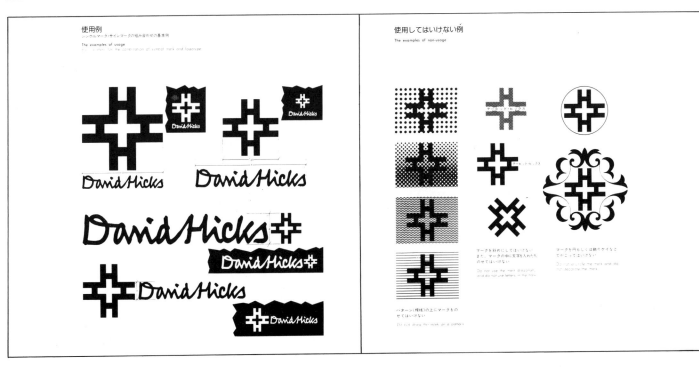

Gardens

□ I do not think that anyone who is not himself a working gardener can have a really good garden. I was brought up in the world of gardening; my mother and father were both very keen on their garden and our gardener and his wife were my best friends when I was a boy. I myself dig, fork, hoe, prune, plant and sow. Many of my ideas have come from what I have seen in other people's gardens – in Japan, India and America as well as in Europe.

□ Planning and planting in a stylish way make up good garden design. It is no use having small groups of plants mixed up together; you must be very bold with your planting. If you have old-fashioned roses,

have a lot of them; the massing of plants is very important. If you have a formal rose bed then make sure that all the roses are the same colour, or at least are planted in blocks of colour.

☐ Design is the essence of a good garden. Gardens should be like houses and have rooms; spaces should be contained by hedges, walls, fences or rows of trees. One of the greatest gardens in the world is at Sissinghurst in Kent, on which the Nicolsons lavished so much love and care. It is a sad thing that when the owners of beautiful houses and gardens depart, most of the character of their gardens disappears very quickly. John Fowler's garden near Odiham had great magic and one hopes that it will survive. Having taken a lot of trouble and care with my garden at Britwell Salome I hope that the new owners will try to maintain it as I did. I am now enjoying planning my new garden – a secret old-rose garden, a spring garden and some *allées*, which are the most rewarding planting of all.

☐ It is very important to choose the right container for one's flowers. I like to vary different flowers with different containers according to the seasons. The more containers you have, of course, the more variety you can achieve.

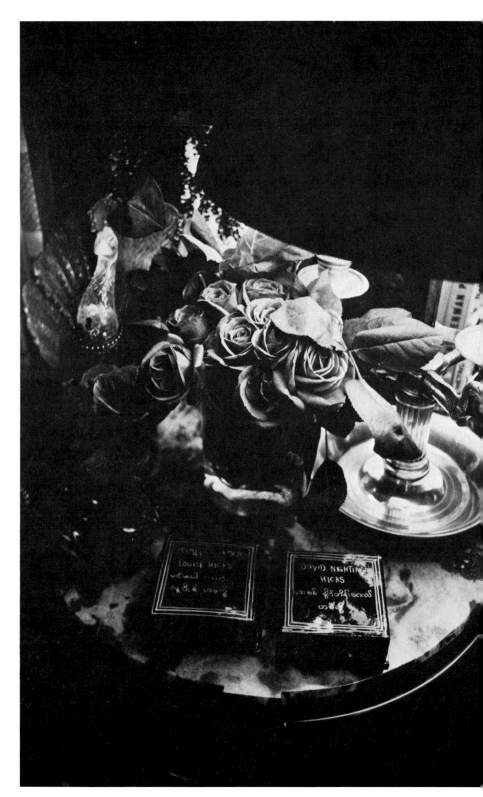

Kitchens

☐ A dramatic kitchen scheme which I designed for an exhibition in black, silver and white using NEFF equipment.

☐ The best food in the world has always come out of kitchens which are somewhat disorganized, untidy and not very planned, and these are the kitchens which usually have the most atmosphere. Kitchens need character, warmth, colour and attractive lighting as much as any other room in the house.
☐ I am as irritated by a kitchen which is over-designed and over-clinical as I am by a kitchen which does not work well. I have a horror of the millionaire house where the owners practically never eat in. Although they have supersonic ovens and dishwashers, a meal from one of these kitchens is pre-cooked and deep-frozen – totally without character. No one wants strawberries all the year round. The best strawberries come straight from the garden and are still warm from the sun.

□ The nicest kitchen I ever had was in my house in the south of France. It was an eighteenth-century one with an early range and *moustière* tiles of the same date. It was dusty, atmospheric and dark and I liked to eat there as much as in the dining-room. The design of a kitchen should enable the room to be used easily and to be as pleasant to eat in as a dining-room.
□ Cynthia Sainsbury is the best amateur cook that I know and how she manages to look divine, to be so witty and produce out of thin air extraordinary food, so effortlessly, I will never know. Richard Chopping and Denis Wirth-Miller have the most attractive kitchen in East Anglia and certainly produce superb results. They are both talented painters and have a great sense of food.

Mirrors

□ Mirror can create a sense of illusion and of space. I use mirror frequently and in a fairly bold way, but one must be careful not to over-use it, for it can create a feeling of vulgarity. It should be used positively but with discretion.

□ Antique mirrors can be very beautiful, but I often use quite plain modern mirror above antique fireplaces; it provides a crisp contrast with a marble or stone fireplace and can produce interesting reflections of other parts of the room. I recently used this

1

reatment on facing chimneys in two rooms which opened into each other with large double doors, and achieved an almost endless series of reflections.
◻ In a Chelsea flat I linked four rooms together using a system of double doors in the corner of each of the farthest rooms covered in mirror which gave an endless enfilade of reflections. My most elaborate use of mirror was in a minute bathroom on Fifth Avenue in New York. I mirrored every single facet of the room, including the ceiling, and created a most intriguing multi-reflected area.

1. Mirror lines an alcove between two units in a bathroom-cum-dressing-room to provide a visual extension to the room; in front of the mirror I placed a day bed in white towelling and some generous cushions.
2. I used stainless steel for the door and architrave of the same room, and clad in mirror an awkward column and the rest of the walls in this vestibule.

Good design is in no way dependent upon money.
I like to spend the minimum of mone

nd yet gain the maximum effect.

Style is not what you do but how you do it.

Good lighting is subtle lighting

Flourescent lighting has r

A seventeenth-century house may have dar

In general, all ceilings and most paintwork in room

282

e more sources of light, the subtler the effect.

ace in the home.

aintwork but rarely a dark ceiling.

hould be white or of a light colour.

Acknowledgements

The majority of the photographs in this book were taken by Jon Harris of Guyatt/Jenkins Design Consultants Ltd.

Additional photographic material was supplied by:
Jean François Aloisi
Jacques Bachmann
M. Berdoy
Christopher Blackwall
Michael Boys
Michael Cook
The Daily Telegraph
(photographer Paul Armiger)
Studio-Dann
M. Guillemot
Ashley Hicks
David Hicks
Nicholas Jenkins
M. Lavrillier
Norman McGrath
Jean-Louis Mennesson
NEFF
Okura Hotel Corp.
J. P. Stevens & Co.

285